THALIA N. ALVAREZ

LET ALL THINGS BE DONE DECENTLY & IN ORDER
I COR 14:40

TABLE OF CONTENTS

Dedication

To My Heavenly Father:

The Author of every good gift and the giver of all creativity. Thank You for entrusting me with the desire and the grace to write this book. I give You all the glory and all the honor. This work belongs to You. Thank You for the early mornings and the late nights, for the quiet moments when You downloaded truth into my spirit, and for the faith to obey when You asked me to write for generations I may never meet. This is Your book, Lord. I surrender it fully into Your hands. Continue to dream through me. Continue to speak through these pages. And may every reader encounter You, the God who restores, heals, and writes the most beautiful love stories.

To My Man Of God, The Love of My Life Victor Benny:

Thank you for your sacrifices,for stepping in with love, helping with the chores, the pickups and drop-offs, and carrying our children to and from their many activities so I could focus on this project. Thank you for carrying our family so faithfully during this season.

Thank you for loving me in every season and every stage of our lives. Thank you for praying with me and for me. I thank the Lord for more than 25 years of growing together, learning together, and choosing to love in order.

This book was birthed from the stages we followed more than two decades ago. What God taught us then, we now get to pour into others, helping them build healthy, God-honoring love stories of their own. You are my answered prayer,my protector, my pastor,

and the steady place God has blessed me with. Thank you for leading with humility, loving with patience, and walking beside me through every season of life. Your prayers, your strength, and your unwavering commitment have shaped our marriage,and this book. I am forever grateful to our Heavenly Father for blessing me with the most precious gift: a man after His own heart. Our marriage has never been perfect, but it has always been healthy.
And that is a testimony of God's grace, Te Amo

To my four beautiful children:

Thank you for your patience and your grace in the many moments I couldn't cook a meal and we had to order in, when laundry waited and socks went missing, and when I was locked away in a room writing. Thank you for the sacrifices you made so I could give birth to these words.

You are my joy, my purpose, and my legacy. Your lives inspire me to grow, to heal, and to pour into others. I pray these words guide you, strengthen you, and prepare you for the godly relationships and marriages God has planned for your future.

To The Reader:

Thank you for opening your heart to this journey. Whether you are single, in friendship, in courtship, engaged, or already married, my prayer is that these pages draw you closer to God's voice, God's timing, and God's beautiful design for love. May the Lord guide your steps, guard your heart, and bless every stage of your story. This book is dedicated with love, gratitude, and prayer for the future God is shaping in your life.

Preface

This book was born out of our own journey, one my husband and I walked step-by-step, stage-by-stage, with God's grace holding us together. We did not learn these stages from a seminar or a conference. We lived them. For many years, we also taught these stages to countless couples, counseling them through the beautiful and challenging seasons of love. We have witnessed many of those couples build successful marriages, notice I said successful, not perfect. Perfection does not exist, but God-given success does.

From friendship, to friends in love, to courtship, to engagement, and now twenty-two years of marriage, we experienced each stage with joy, challenges, tears, laughter, warfare, and incredible growth. We made mistakes, we learned lessons, and we discovered firsthand that God truly cares about every part of a relationship, from the first conversation to the lifelong covenant.

As we were raising our children and began mentoring young adults, we realized how important it is for people to clearly understand these stages. So many relationships fall apart not because of a lack of love, but because people skip steps, misunderstand God's design, or allow emotions to lead instead of the Holy Spirit.

When my daughter began her own courtship journey, the conversations we shared with her brought these principles back to the forefront of my heart and mind. They stirred in me a fresh desire to write this book for the next generation, for those who are praying for love, preparing for marriage, or walking through these stages even now. I wanted to create something that would offer clarity, encouragement, and wisdom.

My hope is that as you read this book, you feel seen, supported, and guided. Whether you are single, in friendship, in courtship, engaged, or already married, may these pages give you peace, direction, and discernment. May they help you avoid unnecessary heartbreak, recognize God's voice above every other voice, and build relationships that truly honor Him. Above all, my prayer is that this book draws you closer to God, the Author of love, the Designer of marriage, and the One who knows how to write the most beautiful stories.

Before we begin exploring the five stages of relationships and learning how to love in order, I want to prepare your heart for what lies ahead. I believe the Holy Spirit desires to walk with you through these pages, not just to inform you, but to transform you.

As you move through this book, you will encounter moments of prayer, reflection, repentance, healing, and forgiveness. These prayers are intentional. They are meant to help you release what no longer belongs in this next season and invite God fully into your journey.

Each stage will guide you step by step, and at the end of every chapter you will find prayers, reflection prompts, and questions designed to help you pause, process, and hear God clearly. This is not a book to rush through, it is a book to walk through with the Lord.

Thank you for trusting the God in me and for choosing this book. This is not just another relationship book. It is a blueprint, God's design for how we are called to love, to walk in purity, and to honor Him in every stage.

This is not a book to rush through. It is a guide meant to be walked through prayerfully and intentionally. Whether you are single, healing, growing, preparing for marriage, or already married, this book is designed to help you love in order, in a healthy and God-centered way.

Let All Things be done decently & in order
1 Cor 14:40

TIME TO HEAL

Psalm 147:3

"He heals the brokenhearted and binds up their wounds."

TIME TO HEAL

A Sacred Pause Before You Continue
Before you turn the page, pause.

If you have experienced pain in past relationships, abuse, betrayal, divorce, manipulation, abandonment, or infidelity, know this truth: God sees you, and God heals. Scripture reminds us, "The Lord is close to the brokenhearted and saves those who are crushed in spirit" (Psalm 34:18).

Healing is not a delay; it is preparation. Too often, people move from relationship to relationship without allowing God to heal the wounds of the past. This section is not about being perfect or fully healed, it is about becoming aware of the places that still hurt and intentionally surrendering them to God.

Healthy, lasting love does not begin with pretending we are whole; it begins with honesty before God. Before continuing this journey, you are invited to bring every broken place to the One who "heals the brokenhearted and binds up their wounds" (Psalm 147:3).

Take a quiet moment now. Ask the Holy Spirit to gently reveal any areas of your heart that still need healing, not to condemn you, but to restore you. Allow His presence to meet you with truth, grace, and compassion.

Entering Prayer and Its Purpose

Prayer is not a ritual, it is an exchange. As you pray, you are releasing what has wounded you and making room for God's healing power to work in your heart. Forgiveness is often the first step in that process. Forgiveness does not excuse what was done to you; it frees you from carrying the weight of it.

Prayer of Forgiveness

Father God,

You ask us to forgive as we have been forgiven. Today, I come to You in obedience and trust, knowing that forgiveness brings freedom.

I choose to forgive ____________________.

I forgive them for ____________________.

Your Word instructs me to release bitterness, anger, and resentment, and to forgive as Christ forgave me (Ephesians 4:31–32). Today, I let go of the pain I have carried, the disappointment, the anger, the grief, and the hurt.

As I stand before You in prayer, I choose forgiveness. I trust that as I release this offense, You will continue the healing work in my heart (Mark 11:25). I place this person and this situation fully into Your hands.

In Jesus' name,

Amen.

Prayer of Healing

Lord Jesus,

You invite the weary and burdened to come to You for rest (Matthew 11:28), and today I come.

I bring every broken piece of my heart to the cross,

every wound I tried to ignore, every pain I normalized, every hurt I buried. You have promised, "I will restore you to health and heal your wounds" (Jeremiah 30:17), and I receive that promise now.

Remove anything in me that has hardened my heart.

Give me a new heart and a new spirit, as You have promised, taking away the heart of stone and replacing it with a heart that is alive, whole, and healed (Ezekiel 36:26).

Heal me where trust was broken.

Deliver me from bitterness, fear, anger, and resentment.

Let the old patterns fall away, for in You I am made new (2 Corinthians 5:17).

In Jesus' name,

Amen.

A Prayer of Release and Renewal

Lord,

I choose not to dwell on what was, for You are doing something new in me (Isaiah 43:18–19). I give You my past, my pain, and my expectations. Teach me to guard my heart with wisdom, knowing that everything in my life flows from it (Proverbs 4:23). I surrender my healing timeline to You and trust that Your restoration is complete and intentional.

I receive Your peace.

I receive Your healing.

I receive Your rest.

In Jesus' name, amen.

Take a deep breath.
Healing is sacred work, and you have just taken a courageous step. As you continue reading, allow love to grow from a heart that is healed, because when the heart is restored, love will always be in order.

Time to Repent
Realigning Your Heart with God's Order
Repentance is not about punishment, it is about realignment.
If at any point you have moved ahead of God's timing...
If you entered relationships without seeking His guidance...
If you pursued intimacy before covenant...
If you allowed desire, loneliness, fear, or pressure to lead you instead of God,
...Then this is a sacred moment to pause and return.

Scripture reminds us that "There is a way that seems right to a person, but its end leads to destruction" (Proverbs 14:12). When we move outside of God's order, confusion, pain, and brokenness often follow. But God, in His mercy, always invites us back.

Repentance simply means to turn back toward God, to acknowledge where we stepped out of alignment and to willingly come under His wisdom once again. "If we confess our sins, He is faithful and just to forgive us and to cleanse us from all unrighteousness" (1 John 1:9).

Take this moment to allow the Holy Spirit to search your heart.

Prayer of Repentance

Father God,

I come before You with humility and honesty.

I acknowledge the moments where I moved ahead of You, where I followed my own understanding instead of trusting You (Proverbs 3:5–6). I confess that I entered relationships without Your direction and made choices outside of Your timing and Your order. Forgive me for placing my desires above Your will. Forgive me for opening doors You never asked me to walk through.

I turn away from every relationship, habit, and decision that was not led by You.

Your Word calls me to seek first Your kingdom and Your righteousness (Matthew 6:33), and today I choose to realign my heart with Yours.

In Jesus' name,

Amen.

Let All Things be done decently & in order
1 Cor 14:40

INTRODUCTION

INTRODUCTION:
Walking Through the Stages with God

There was a time when I believed love was simple, just like the movies. You meet the right person, fall deeply in love, and suddenly life feels perfect. You're walking hand in hand, talking for hours, and feeling butterflies with every glance. Then the story closes with birds circling the sky, the screen turns golden, and bold letters appear saying "Happily Ever After," as if romance alone could carry the whole story.

But as time passed, I learned that real relationships don't end at the credits. Life keeps going long after the butterflies fade. Emotions shift, responsibilities grow, and the true foundation of a relationship begins to show. That's when I discovered something important: love cannot be built on feelings alone, it must be shaped by God's timing, God's wisdom, and God's purpose.

Every stage of a relationship carries lessons uniquely designed to prepare us for what comes next. Each stage is beautiful in its own way, filled with moments that shape our character and strengthen our faith. And no matter where you find yourself today, know this, God is walking with you. Your story was written by Him before you were born. When you seek Him in every stage, He guides your heart with peace, clarity, and direction.

We live in a world that rushes everything: relationships, emotions, decisions, and commitment. But Scripture reminds us, "To everything there is a season, and a time to every purpose under heaven" (Ecclesiastes 3:1). Rushing ahead only brings confusion, but moving in God's timing brings alignment, strength, and purpose.

This book is written to help you recognize those stages. Think of it as a road map to a godly relationship, a guide to help you understand what God may be doing in your heart and life right now. It's not just about gaining knowledge. It's about walking hand in hand with the Holy Spirit, allowing Him to shape you, prepare you, and lead you with patience and discernment.

In Scripture, the tribe of Issachar was known for their ability to discern seasons. The Bible says they "understood the times and knew what Israel should do" (1 Chronicles 12:32). They recognized the timing. They were spiritually sensitive to what God was doing. This same wisdom is vital in relationships, because when you know what season you're in, you know how to respond.

My husband once preached a message that captured this beautifully. He said, "You have to be dressed for the right weather. You can't wear summer clothes in the winter, and you can't wear winter clothes in the summer." When you don't know your season, you end up unprepared, uncomfortable, or even exposed. The same is true in our love lives. When we try to act like we're in a "marriage season" while God still has us in a "friendship season," frustration and disappointment follow. But when we align ourselves with God's timing, everything becomes clearer.

The Bible tells us that God orders our steps (Psalm 37:23) and that He makes everything beautiful in its time (Ecclesiastes 3:11). Nothing in our lives is random, and no stage is wasted. Every stage has a purpose. Our responsibility is to hear His voice, recognize His timing, and allow Him to lead, so we can walk forward with wisdom, clarity, and peace instead of rushing ahead in emotion or fear. Each chapter of this book represents a season, a stage, and a step in the journey toward the relationship God desires for you.

Stage 1: Friendship – The foundation of trust, safety, and faith.

Stage 2: Friends in Love – The gentle awakening of deeper connection.

Stage 3: Courtship – Choosing each other with intention and honoring God together.

Stage 4: Engagement – Preparing your hearts and minds for covenant.

Stage 5: Marriage – The fulfillment of God's design and the beginning of a new story.

My prayer is that as you read these pages, you will slow down, reflect deeply, and invite God into every part of your journey. Whether you are waiting, healing, growing, or preparing for marriage, hold this truth close: God's timing is perfect, and He is faithfully writing your story. His plan for your love, your relationship, and your future is far greater than anything you could ever imagine.

"Now to Him who is able to do exceedingly abundantly above all that we ask or think, according to the power that works in us."
Ephesians 3:20

BEFORE WE DIVE IN:
The Importance of Hearing God's Voice

Before we move into the stages of a relationship, I want to give you wisdom that is absolutely vital. The beginning of any relationship is a delicate time. Emotions rise quickly, attachments form easily, and judgment can become cloudy if you are not anchored in the voice of God. Relationships, especially in their early stages, require spiritual sensitivity and discernment.

This is why it is essential to listen to God's voice above every other voice. Be careful with prophetic words, impressions, dreams, and emotions. God still speaks through all of these, but not everything we feel or hear is from Him. Scripture tells us to "test the spirits"

(1 John 4:1) and to examine every word carefully. Never allow a prophecy, a dream, or someone else's opinion to replace your personal relationship with God. In every season, especially in relationships, God's voice must be stronger, clearer, and louder than any other voice in your life.

MY STORY:
Following God When Others Disagreed

When I met the man who would one day become my husband, we had a long-distance relationship. At the time I lived in Puerto Rico, and he lived in New York. After praying for about a year, we both felt God leading me to move to New York. But once I shared this, the voices around me grew loud.

Some people questioned my decision, and others openly disagreed. One of the pastors at the church I attended at the time told me, *"You are not leaving to New York."* On another occasion, I remember sitting in a room with the youth leaders as they shared their desire for me to lead the dance ministry. Accepting that role would have required me to stay in Puerto Rico, and it was a ministry I absolutely loved with all my heart.

Their words and their offer created deep confusion within me. My spirit knew what God had spoken, but my flesh wrestled with the fear of disappointing people and walking away from something familiar. But I obeyed the Lord and moved to New York.

And let me tell you, the opposition did not stop there. Leaders from the church my boyfriend attended during our courtship began saying that our relationship was not from God. It wasn't just one person, it was several. Looking back, I thank the Lord for the strong relationship we both had (and still have) with our Heavenly Father. It was our own intimate relationship with God that anchored us when people's opinions tried to shake us.

We held onto what God had confirmed to both of us, even when it was hard. I remember feeling alone, I was in a new state, new culture and a new church. But one thing we did was pray in secret, and God rewarded us openly. Today, by the grace of God, as I write this book, we have been married 22 years.

Through this experience, I learned something powerful: We do not fight against flesh and blood (Ephesians 6:12).
- You don't fight with people—you pray.
- You don't take it personally—you pray.
- You don't fight in the natural—you fight in the spiritual.

Let me pause here for clarity, so there is no confusion or misunderstanding that could be taken as encouraging rebellion or a refusal to listen to parents or leaders.

Obedience matters. Submission to God matters. Discernment matters. You must make sure you are genuinely walking in obedience to the Holy Spirit. Do not call rebellion "faith," and do not use "God told me" as an excuse to pursue something your flesh desires. Seek God sincerely, humbly, and consistently.

And hear my heart: if you are with someone who is not walking with God, not aligned with your faith, or pulling you away spiritually, you should end that relationship. Anything that takes you away from God's presence or God's purpose can become an idol. If God is telling you to let that person go, be obedient and trust that He will provide the right person at the right time. The Bible is clear, you cannot be unequally yoked (2 Corinthians 6:14). Alignment with God's will and His Word is essential.

A STORY OF DISCERNMENT:
When God Says "No"

$\mathcal{I}$ want to share a quick story about a friend. We'll call them Janet and Joel. Janet had been close friends with a man named Joel for several years. One day, Joel expressed that he wanted to move their friendship, Stage One, into something deeper. They are now entering Stage Two: Friends in Love, where romantic feelings begin to awaken. Everyone around Janet was excited for her... but Janet wasn't.

She kept saying, "I don't think he's the one, but I'm going to pray."

As they both prayed for God's confirmation, the Lord began speaking to Janet through a series of dreams, showing her clearly that Joel was not her husband. After a few months, Janet had peace about what God was telling her. She knew it was time to share the truth.

She told Joel, "We need to stop praying for confirmation about this relationship. God already spoke to me, *you are not the one.*"

Joel became upset and said, "I'm going to keep praying because I know what God said. God told me you're the one for me."

A few years down the line Joel married someone else, and Janet married the man God truly had for her. Today, they are both happily married to the spouses God prepared for them. Twenty-something years later, they are still friends, and we all still get to joke about it. Unfortunately, not many stories end this way.

When people do not listen to God, they often end up in toxic relationships, hurt and wounded.

Their story shows how emotions can easily cause confusion, especially in friendships. This is why wisdom and discernment are vital in this process. This is not an easy walk in the park. It's a major life decision, and it's one you want God to lead rather than your emotions. Emotional clarity matters. That is why you should never allow someone else's "God told me" to guide your life. Instead, seeking God's voice through prayer, fasting, and asking God for confirmation is essential.

We see the importance of confirmation in Scripture.

In Genesis 24, Abraham's servant traveled to find a wife for Isaac. He didn't make assumptions. He didn't move by emotion. He asked God for a clear sign, a woman who would offer water to him and to his camels. He prayed *in silence*, and God answered *with clarity*. Rebekah appeared, fulfilling every detail of his prayer. This reminds us that: Asking for confirmation is biblical; however, you don't need to announce to people what confirmation you're asking for; this is between you and God.

Joel and Janet never let emotions, pressure, excitement, or another person's "word from God" dictate their decisions.

If someone says, *"God told me you're my spouse,"* but God has not spoken to you... Your job is going to be PRAY PRAY, and again I say, PRAY!

God is faithful to reveal His will to anyone who seeks Him with a sincere, surrendered heart. God does not move in confusion, He moves in clarity.

If He is in it — He will confirm it.
If He is not in it — He will protect you from it.

Let All Things be done decently & in order
1 Cor 14:40

STAGE 1: FRIENDSHIP

THE FOUNDATION OF A GODLY RELATIONSHIP

JOHN 15:13

GREATER LOVE HAS NO ONE THAN THIS: TO LAY DOWN ONE'S LIFE FOR ONE'S FRIENDS.

STAGE 1: FRIENDSHIP
The Foundation of a Godly Relationship

When I was in elementary school, I remember having friends who were boys, and the moment anyone even talked to the opposite gender, especially during recess,the teasing would begin. My classmates would break out into that famous playground rhyme, and many times I joined in too. You probably know it; it goes like this:

"___ and ___ sitting in a tree,

K-I-S-S-I-N-G.

First comes love, then comes marriage,

Then comes the baby in the baby carriage!"

We laughed, giggled, and teased each other, never realizing how much is truly missing from this rhyme. Because in real life, before the K-I-S-S-I-N-G, before the "love," before the marriage, and long before the baby carriage... There is something far more important: Friendship.

Friendship is God's true beginning. It is the steady, safe, intentional place where two hearts learn each other without pressure, without expectations, and without rushing ahead of His timing. Before romance, before feelings, before dreams of marriage, there is friendship.

WHY FRIENDSHIP MATTERS

As you read earlier in the story of Joel and Janet, their journey shows how easily emotions can cause confusion, especially in friendships. This is why wisdom and discernment are vital in this process. This is **not** an easy walk in the park. It's a major life decision, and it's one you want God to lead rather than your emotions. Emotional clarity matters. That is why you should never allow someone else's "God told me" to guide your life. Instead, seeking God's voice through prayer, fasting, and asking God for confirmation is essential.

Scripture teaches us that two people must be aligned before they can walk in unity. Amos 3:3 says, "Can two walk together, unless they are agreed?"

Friendship is the place where alignment begins, emotionally, spiritually, and mentally. It is where you learn whether your values, faith, and life goals match.

Friendship comes before partnership.
Before a relationship can move forward, unity must already exist. Friendship allows you to see whether you can truly walk together in agreement (Amos 3:3).

Before love is built, friendship must be tested.
True friendship is proven over time, not in perfect moments but in real ones. Proverbs 17:17 says, "A friend loves at all times, and a brother is born for adversity." This means a genuine friend shows consistency, loyalty, and love, even in difficulty. Romance can hide flaws, but friendship reveals truth.

Before hearts are joined, spirits must be aligned

Scripture is clear that spiritual alignment is vital. 2 Corinthians 6:14 warns, "Do not be unequally yoked with unbelievers." Friendship exposes whether someone's relationship with God matches yours. It protects you from connecting with someone who may draw you away from God instead of toward Him.

Before purpose is pursued, character must be revealed

Real character is not seen in romance, it is seen in friendship. Proverbs 27:17 says, "As iron sharpens iron, so one person sharpens another." Friendship is where refinement happens. It is where you observe integrity, honesty, discipline, and humility. Before God joins two purposes together, He uses friendship to reveal who someone truly is.

God uses friendship to protect your heart and reveal truth

Friendships often show warning signs long before emotions cloud your judgment. Proverbs 13:20 says, "Walk with the wise and become wise, for a companion of fools suffers harm." The people you walk closely with will influence your direction. And Ecclesiastes 4:9–10 reminds us that friendship is God's gift of support and accountability: *Two are better than one... If either of them falls, one can help the other up.* " Friendship is God's safety net. It gives you room to observe, discern, and hear God clearly before your heart becomes deeply attached. It reveals someone's fruit, their spiritual maturity, and their priorities long before deeper feelings take root.

WHAT A GODLY FRIENDSHIP LOOKS LIKE

A Godly friendship begins with respect. Respect for boundaries, feelings, time, values, and personal space. Respect honors the whole person and creates safety. It says, "I value who you are, not just what you offer."

Honesty is equally essential. Open, transparent communication builds trust and allows connection to deepen without fear of judgment. Godly friends speak truth with love and create a safe place for vulnerability.

True friendship also produces support and encouragement. Real friends uplift each other spiritually, emotionally, and mentally. They help each other grow into the people God has called them to be. Proverbs 27:9 says, *"The heartfelt counsel of a friend is as sweet as perfume and incense."* God sends the right friends to sharpen, strengthen, and support your walk with Him.

Purity plays an important role as well. When a friendship remains Christ-centered, it develops naturally and with integrity, without pressure, flirtation, or the temptation of premature intimacy. Purity keeps the connection clean, healthy, and protected.

And then there is patience, one of the most overlooked yet most important elements. Godly friendships take time. Patience allows the relationship to grow in God's timing, not emotional impulse. Anything rushed is rarely rooted.

A true friendship prepares the heart for deeper commitment. It gives you space to observe character over time without the distortion of romantic emotion. This is where trust forms, shared values take root, and spiritual unity begins to develop. Friendship is where emotional and spiritual bonding begins long before love awakens.

WHAT A GODLY FRIENDSHIP IS NOT

 Now that we've explored what a Godly friendship *is*, it is just as important to understand what a Godly friendship *is not*. We live in a culture that has distorted the meaning of relationship and blurred the lines between friendship, dating, and emotional attachment. Because of this, many people unknowingly step into connections that look harmless on the surface, but spiritually they are damaging.

One of the most common counterfeits to true friendship is what culture calls "friends with benefits." Movies, music, and society normalize the idea of being "just friends" while engaging in physical affection, flirting, kissing, sexual touching, or even sexual intimacy. But this is not friendship, this is confusion. Scripture clearly calls us to purity, instructing us to "run from sexual sin" (1 Corinthians 6:18). Any connection that mimics the behaviors of marriage or dating without covenant creates emotional attachment God never intended. It steals clarity, damages trust, and deeply wounds the heart.

Another counterfeit is a friendship filled with mixed signals, when someone treats you like a partner one day and ignores you the next, flirts but refuses to commit, or keeps you emotionally close while leaving other options open. This kind of instability is not godly friendship; it is emotional manipulation. The Bible teaches us, "Let your 'Yes' be 'Yes,' and your 'No,' 'No'" (Matthew 5:37). True friendship is consistent, honest, and steady, not confusing or unpredictable.

A friendship also becomes unhealthy when it turns into emotional dependence. Sometimes two people become so connected that one becomes the other's emotional lifeline, sharing deep vulnerability, trauma, fears, and personal needs in a way that should be reserved for covenant, not friendship. When this happens, an ungodly emotional soul tie begins to form. Soul ties develop when time, vulnerability, affection, and emotional dependency bind two hearts together in a way that bypasses God's order and protection. Godly friendships strengthen you, but unhealthy emotional ties drain you and create attachment outside of God's will.

Another form of counterfeit friendship is hidden romantic attachment. If one person is secretly hoping for more, acting like a boyfriend or girlfriend, or forming romantic expectations without communication or clarity, this is not friendship. It is an emotional entanglement. God is not the author of confusion but of peace (1 Corinthians 14:33). If confusion is present, God is not at the center.

Finally, friendship is not a disguise for disobedience. Sometimes people claim, "We're just friends," while holding hands, cuddling, flirting, or engaging in behaviors that belong to a covenant relationship. This is not friendship; this is rebellion wrapped in excuses. Scripture warns us not to "use your freedom as a cover-up for evil" (1 Peter 2:16). Godly friendship honors boundaries. Anything that secretly imitates dating while denying commitment is not God's design.

A counterfeit friendship always carries three signs:
confusion, compromise, and emotional instability.

A Godly friendship carries three very different signs:
clarity, purity, and peace.

If someone in your life calls themselves a "friend," yet wants the benefits of romance, kissing, touching, sexual intimacy, emotional dependence, or private conversations that imitate a relationship, that is not friendship. And if *you* have allowed a connection like this to continue under the label of "friendship," understand this with love: that space is not safe for your heart. It is where confusion grows, soul ties form, and the enemy plants counterfeits that distract you from what God truly has for you.

Anything God builds begins with clarity and truth.
Anything the enemy builds begins with confusion and compromise.

A God-centered friendship will protect your purity, guard your heart, and prepare you for the relationship God has designed for you. Your heart was not created for confusion. It was created for peace. And peace is always the fruit of God's presence.

A WARNING ABOUT UNGODLY SOUL TIES

So far in this chapter, you've learned about the foundation of friendship, why friendship matters, what a godly friendship is, and what it is not. Now I want to take you a little deeper, because understanding this next part will protect your heart for the rest of your life.

Have you ever been in a relationship where you told yourself, *"It's over,"* yet you still felt drawn back?

Have you ever tried to walk away, but something inside you kept pulling you toward a person you knew was not good for you?

Have you ever felt emotionally tied to someone long after the relationship ended?

That pull is not romance.
It is not "chemistry."
It is not "closure."
It is a soul tie.

Many people think soul ties only happen with sex. They do not. Emotional vulnerability, intimate conversations, unhealthy dependence, or repeated cycles of breaking up and returning can all form a spiritual tie that binds the heart in ways God never intended.

And hear me clearly:
Ungodly soul ties can form in any stage, even in marriage. My husband and I learned this the hard way.

OUR PERSONAL EXPERIENCE WITH SOUL TIES

One of the ways my husband and I like to teach is based on our own experiences . Both my husband and I have lived through this, and we share it so that you will never have to walk blindly through something that almost destroyed us.

MY STORY

My soul tie experience happened in the early years of our marriage. I traveled alone to Puerto Rico to visit my family, and during that trip, I ran into an ex-boyfriend from my teenage years. We exchanged numbers, thinking it was "innocent," but what seemed harmless began to stir old emotions.

When I returned to New York, I found myself constantly talking to him while at work. We were emailing back and forth, and even though I knew in my spirit it was wrong, I felt unable to stop. There was a pull, a connection , that clouded my judgment.

Meanwhile, my husband could feel that something was off. I had become distant, withdrawn, and emotionally unavailable. He is a Godly man, sensitive to the Holy Spirit, and he felt the shift immediately.

When the truth came to light, we sought prayer and counsel from our youth pastors. We fasted. We cried. We fought spiritually. And God broke that soul tie completely.

What shocked me was that I had not kissed or hugged this person, there was no physical contact at all. It seemed like an innocent conversation and a simple exchange of phone numbers, yet I learned emotional ties can form long before physical boundaries are crossed. I opened an emotional door that should have remained closed. The enemy will use the smallest crack to try to destroy what God has built. It is important to recognize small compromises before they become strongholds.

MY HUSBAND'S STORY

My husband also experienced an ungodly soul tie, but his looked different. He had a long-time female friend, whom he grew up with in the Lord. Even after we were married, they would be on the phone for hours having long conversations. They were never inappropriate, but they were emotionally close. I would even join the conversations at times because everything seemed harmless.

But when we were anointed as pastors, the Lord spoke clearly to both of us that boundaries with the opposite sex needed to change. We agreed that from that point on, neither of us would text or call people of the opposite sex unless our spouse was included in the conversation. The moment that boundary was set, everything was exposed.

This friend continued texting my husband without including me. Even after he reminded her to add me, she resisted the change. One day, in prayer, the Lord revealed to me that the connection between them, though never physical or romantic, had become a soul tie.

Breaking that tie was not easy emotionally, but once it was severed, our marriage entered a new level of unity, clarity, and peace.

SO WHAT EXACTLY IS A SOUL TIE?

Biblically, a soul tie is a deep emotional, spiritual, or physical bond that connects you to another person in a way that begins to influence your thoughts, your feelings, and even your decisions. God designed soul ties for covenant relationships, marriage, godly friendships, and family, bonds that strengthen, protect, and align you with His purpose. But the enemy loves to imitate what God creates.

An ungodly soul tie forms when a connection develops outside of God's order. It binds you in a way that clouds your judgment, weakens spiritual discernment, stirs temptation, creates emotional confusion, and keeps you attached to someone God never approved. It doesn't bless you, it binds you. It doesn't lift you, it drains you. It doesn't lead you closer to God, it pulls you away. Ungodly soul ties do not bring freedom; they bring spiritual fog, emotional unrest, and disconnection from God's voice.

HOW SOUL TIES FORM

A soul tie forms when two people connect on a deep level through emotional intimacy, repeated vulnerability, constant communication, dependency, physical affection or sexual activity, cycles of breaking up and returning, or through secret conversations and hidden expectations.

These moments may seem harmless in the beginning, but they quietly create spiritual bonds, attachments that often remain active long after the relationship has ended.

This is why so many people say:
"I know he isn't good for me...

but I can't stop thinking about him."
or
"We broke up, but something always pulls me back."

That pull is not love. It is a soul tie.

Ungodly soul ties lead to confusion, heartbreak, spiritual warfare, and difficulty moving forward. Judgment becomes clouded. Boundaries weaken. Emotions override discernment. Your spiritual walk suffers because your heart is tied to a place God never prepared for you.

This is why friendship must remain pure, honest, and clearly defined. Any emotional or physical intimacy outside of God's order creates bondage, not blessing.

If You Find Yourself in an Ungodly Connection…

- Maybe you are in a confusing "friendship."
- Maybe you are emotionally entangled with someone who is not yours.
- Maybe it's a "friends-with-benefits" situation you know is wrong.
- Maybe you left the relationship, but your heart never did.

If so, hear this with love:
Pause. Seek God. Set boundaries. Break the ungodly tie.

You do not need to carry shame. You do not need to condemn yourself or anyone else. But you do need to surrender the connection to God so He can bring healing, clarity, and freedom.

Your heart is too precious, your purpose too great, and your future too valuable to be tied to anything, or anyone, God did not ordain.

You have learned what friendship *is* and what it is *not*.
You have learned how godly connections strengthen you, and how ungodly ties can distract, confuse, or even harm your heart.

But the good news is:
God restores.
God realigns.
God rebuilds.
And God prepares your heart for the right relationships.

As you move toward Stage Two — *Friends in Love* — remember this truth:
Every healthy love story begins with a healthy friendship.

When the foundation is strong, the transition into love becomes clear, peaceful, and God-led. Before we step into Stage Two, take a moment to reflect and let God speak to your heart.
As we end this chapter on friendship, remember this, Godly friendship:

- is not accidental, it is intentional, protected, and built on truth.
- honors God, it guards the heart, and it prepares you for everything that will come in the stages ahead.

PRAYERS FOR STAGE 1: FRIENDSHIP

Prayer for Friendship & Heart Alignment

Lord, thank You for the gift of friendship. Teach me how to be a godly friend, one who loves with purity, truth, honor, and patience. Surround me with friendships that strengthen my walk with You and remove anything that is not from You. Protect my heart, purify my motives, and align my relationships with Your will. Prepare me for the next stage of my journey, and help me walk in wisdom, discernment, and peace. In Jesus name, Amen.

Prayer for Breaking Soul Ties

Father, in the name of Jesus, I surrender every unhealthy attachment, emotional, spiritual, or physical, that is not from You. I renounce every ungodly soul tie, every connection that has clouded my judgment, weakened my spirit, or pulled me away from Your purpose. By the power of the Holy Spirit, break every tie that does not honor You. Restore my heart, renew my mind, and align my desires with Your perfect will. I receive freedom, clarity, and healing today. In Jesus name, Amen.

REFLECTION QUESTIONS

Take time to sit with these questions in prayer:

1. Are my current friendships bringing me closer to God or pulling me away?

2. Have I been calling something "friendship" that God is calling confusion?

3. Am I respecting boundaries, emotionally, spiritually, and physically?

4.   Do I see Christlike character in the friendships I'm investing in?

5. Are there any unhealthy attachments or soul ties affecting my heart, clarity, or peace?

6. Have I been honest with God and myself, about relationships I need to let go of?

Let All Things be done decently & in order
1 Cor 14:40

STAGE 2: FRIENDS IN LOVE

THE BIRTH OF ROMANTIC FEELINGS

PROVERBS 17:17

A FRIEND LOVES AT ALL TIMES...

STAGE 2: FRIENDS IN LOVE
The Birth of Romantic Feelings

When Friendship Begins to Blossom Into Something More After a friendship has been firmly established, something beautiful often begins to happen, romantic feelings start to grow. Stage Two, Friends in Love, is an exciting season filled with anticipation and tenderness, but it is also emotionally and spiritually delicate.

One of the best ways to understand this stage is by comparing it to the first trimester of pregnancy. In the early weeks, everything is fragile, tender, and still hidden. New life is forming, but it requires great care and protection. In the same way, when romantic feelings first begin to develop, they must be guarded with wisdom, prayer, and emotional maturity.

Just as a pregnant woman protects the life growing within her, the early stages of romantic affection should be handled gently and intentionally. This is not a season to rush, expose, or overexplain. It is a season to nurture what is forming while seeking God for clarity and direction.

This is why I strongly recommend praying and moving in silence during Stage Two. What does that mean? It means you do not announce these new feelings to everyone or broadcast them on social media. If necessary, you may share with your parents or a trusted mentor, but keep the circle small. Anything in its early development is vulnerable.

The enemy often seeks to disrupt what God is quietly trying to build. Just as a woman protects her womb during the early months of pregnancy, you must protect the beginnings of romantic affection through prayer, fasting, discernment, and discretion.

Many people say, *"I need to date around to see if he's the one,"* but that is not always true. This is precisely why Stage Two—Friends in Love—exists. It is the natural space where affection can be acknowledged, discerned, and surrendered to God, *without rushing into commitment or attaching prematurely.*

Stage Two allows you to observe, pray, and seek clarity before moving forward. It creates room for God to reveal alignment,or misalignment, while hearts are still protected and emotions remain grounded in wisdom rather than impulse.

Understanding the Shift: When Friendship Becomes Something More

After the foundation of friendship has been established, Stage Two is where both individuals begin to sense that the connection is deepening. Romantic feelings may begin to form, and admiration gradually transitions into affection. This can be an exciting stage, but it must be handled with intention, prayer, and emotional maturity.

Romantic feelings often develop naturally, but they must be guided spiritually. This stage requires awareness and discernment. Pay attention to the internal shifts. Notice when your heart begins to respond differently. Rather than reacting impulsively, bring your emotions before God. Ask Him whether this growing affection aligns with His purpose and timing.

As feelings begin to arise, they should be approached with honest and respectful conversations. Clear communication helps clarify intentions, set healthy boundaries, and keep both hearts aligned. Stage Two is not about rushing toward commitment, it is about understanding what is unfolding and discerning whether it should move forward.

WHEN ATTRACTION IS CENTERED ON GOD

When attraction is genuinely centered on God, it develops in an atmosphere of safety, honor, and peace. It produces spiritual fruit, emotional stability, mutual respect, clarity, joy, holiness, and purpose.

A God-centered attraction does not steal your peace, pressure you into compromise, or destabilize your emotions. It does not pull you away from God or create confusion within your spirit. Instead, it draws you closer to Him, strengthens your walk, and prepares both hearts for whatever He desires to build next.

This is why Stage Two requires discernment, because not every feeling is meant to be followed, but every feeling is meant to be surrendered to God.

PRAYER IS ESSENTIAL

Boundaries become especially important here. Protecting your heart means resisting the urge to rush ahead or make decisions based solely on emotion. And this is where prayer becomes absolutely essential.

During this stage, there is no physical affection, no holding hands, no kissing, no blurring emotional lines. This season is about prayer, clarity, and seeking God's voice. You are both asking God individually and together, "Is this Your will?" Take intentional time to pray alone, to fast, and to surrender your feelings before the Lord. If both of you feel led, you can even fast together and pray over the phone.

People often ask, "How long does this stage last?"

The truth is, there is no set timeline. It depends entirely on how God chooses to speak to you both about the relationship. The purpose of Stage Two is not speed, it's spiritual confirmation.

Entering this season without God opens the door to confusion, misalignment, and unnecessary emotional pain. Feelings rise quickly. Hopes grow fast. Without the Holy Spirit leading you, it becomes easy to attach yourself to someone who may not be God's will for you.

In This Tender Stage, Ask God For Four Things:

1. **Discernment:**

Discernment is spiritual insight. It's the ability to recognize what is from God and what is not. "Trust in the Lord with all your heart... and He will direct your paths." Proverbs 3:5–6

2. **Patience**

Patience keeps you aligned with God's timing instead of your emotions.

"Wait for the Lord; be strong and take heart." Psalm 27:14

3. **Protection**

Protection means guarding your heart from premature attachment.

"Above all else, guard your heart..." Proverbs 4:23

4. **Clarity**

God speaks clearly to His children; confusion is not His voice.

"For God is not the author of confusion, but of peace." 1 Corinthians 14:33

RELEASING SOMEONE IN STAGE TWO IS NOT FAILURE, IT IS PROTECTION.

Releasing someone in Stage Two is not failure; it is protection. As you read in the opening of this book through the story of Janet and Joel, this stage exists to help you discern early—before emotions deepen and attachments form. What Janet chose in Stage Two was not rejection; it was obedience.

Stage Two is designed to reveal truth, not to force connection. When God shows you that something is misaligned, honoring that revelation is an act of wisdom and self-respect. Emotional interest alone is not confirmation, and chemistry is not a substitute for clarity.

Releasing someone at this stage does not mean you failed, missed God, or walked away too soon. It means you listened. It means you trusted God enough to pause instead of pushing forward. Just as Janet did with Joel, choosing to release is sometimes the most faithful decision you can make.

When something is misaligned, God often reveals it early; not to hurt you, but to protect you. Choosing to release what does not carry His peace preserves your heart, guards your future, and keeps you aligned with His will. It is okay to release someone in Stage Two. Doing so honors God's order and creates space for what He truly intends.

RED FLAGS IN STAGE TWO
God Often Reveals Misalignment Early to Protect Your Heart

Stage Two is a season of discernment. God often reveals misalignment early—not to confuse you, but to protect your heart. Pay attention to the warning signs. Red flags are not meant to create fear; they are invitations to pause, pray, and seek wisdom.

Watch For The Following:

Pressure to Move Fast
Love is patient. Pressure to rush emotional or physical intimacy is a warning sign.
"Love is patient..." (1 Corinthians 13:4)

Jealousy or Controlling Behavior
Possessiveness is rooted in insecurity, not love. Healthy love honors freedom and trust.
"Love... is not self-seeking." (1 Corinthians 13:5)

Emotional Dependence
A romantic interest should never replace God as your source of security, peace, or identity.
"Truly my soul finds rest in God alone." (Psalm 62:1)

Spiritual Inconsistency

Uneven spiritual maturity often creates confusion, imbalance, and division over time.

"Can two walk together unless they are agreed?" (Amos 3:3)

Unclear Intentions

God values clarity. Vague communication and mixed signals lead to confusion, not peace.

"Let your 'Yes' be 'Yes,' and your 'No,' 'No.'" (Matthew 5:37)

Secrecy or Dishonesty

Trust cannot grow in secrecy. What requires hiding often lacks alignment.

"The Lord detests lying lips, but He delights in people who are trustworthy." (Proverbs 12:22)

Disrupted Peace

If peace consistently disappears, it is a sign that something requires prayer and attention.

"Let the peace of Christ rule in your hearts." (Colossians 3:15)

HOW TO NAVIGATE STAGE 2:

This stage requires intentionality and spiritual awareness. Above all, keep God at the center of every thought, conversation, and decision. Scripture reminds us, *"In all your ways acknowledge Him, and He shall direct your paths"* (Proverbs 3:6). When God is acknowledged first, He provides direction, clarity, and peace for every step ahead.

Guard your heart carefully, because emotions rise quickly in this stage, and what you protect now will shape what follows. The Bible instructs us, *"Above all else, guard your heart, for everything you do flows from it"* (Proverbs 4:23). Protecting your heart is not about fear—it is about wisdom, discernment, and stewardship of what God is developing within you.

Clear and honest communication is essential. Clarity builds trust and prevents confusion, allowing both hearts to remain aligned. Jesus teaches, *"Let your 'Yes' be 'Yes,' and your 'No,' 'No.' Anything more than this comes from the evil one"* (Matthew 5:37). God-honoring relationships are rooted in honesty, transparency, and integrity.

Even as feelings grow, continue nurturing the friendship that brought you here. Friendship remains the foundation, and love rooted in friendship is strengthened by loyalty, patience, and consistency. Scripture reminds us, *"A friend loves at all times, and a brother is born for a time of adversity"* (Proverbs 17:17).

Do not walk this season alone. Seek godly counsel from wise mentors who can offer wisdom, prayer, and accountability. The Word reminds us, *"Plans fail for lack of counsel, but with many advisers they succeed"* (Proverbs 15:22).

Finally, move slowly and intentionally. Waiting on the Lord is not a delay, it is an act of wisdom and trust. Scripture encourages us, *"Be still before the Lord and wait patiently for Him"* (Psalm 37:7). When you trust God's timing, He brings peace, confirmation, and clear direction.

PRAYER FOR STAGE 2:
FRIENDS IN LOVE

Father,

I bring my heart and emotions before You in this season. Thank You for the gift of connection and the beauty of growing affection. Help me to walk wisely, move slowly, and listen closely to your voice.

Guard my heart, align my desires with Your will, and give me discernment beyond my emotions. Teach me to trust Your timing, honor Your order, and obey You even when waiting feels difficult.

If this connection is from You, let it grow with peace and clarity. If it is not, give me the courage to release it with grace and trust that You are protecting me. I surrender every feeling, hope, and expectation to You.

In Jesus name, Amen.

REFLECTION QUESTIONS

Take time to sit with these questions in prayer:

1. Are my feelings being guided by God's wisdom, or by my own desires and emotions?

2. Am I willing to wait for God's timing, even if it requires patience or slowing down?

3. Am I seeking God's confirmation, or am I relying on emotion alone to move forward?

STAGE 3: COURTSHIP

THE BIRTH OF ROMANTIC FEELINGS

ECCLESIASTES 3:1

THERE IS A TIME FOR EVERYTHING, AND A SEASON FOR EVERY ACTIVITY UNDER THE HEAVENS.

STAGE 3: COURTSHIP
Honoring the Relationship Before God

*C*ourtship is the stage that comes after God has spoken. It happens after friendship has taken root and romantic interest has been confirmed through prayer, peace, and clarity. This is the moment when two people acknowledge that what they share is not casual and not accidental. Courtship is intentional, sacred, and marked by a shared desire to honor God.

What sets this apart from the world's view of dating is its covenantal aim. In the Bible, marriage, salvation, and God's promises are described as covenants. A covenant is a holy bond not rooted in convenience or emotion, but in commitment and faithfulness.

It is a season where both individuals commit to protecting one another spiritually, emotionally, and physically while seeking God's will for marriage. Courtship is not simply preparing for a wedding. It is preparing for a covenant, a sacred God- ordained relationship. Making God the Center of the Relationship

A godly courtship cannot thrive unless God is at the center. When God leads the relationship, clarity replaces confusion, peace replaces anxiety, and purpose replaces pressure. Courtship is not sustained by emotions alone, it is sustained by surrender.

Anything God ordains, the enemy opposes. When a relationship begins moving toward covenant, spiritual pressure often increases. Confusion, temptation, fear, insecurity, unnecessary arguments, and emotional distractions may arise, not because something is wrong, but because something is right.

This is why courtship requires spiritual maturity. When God has spoken, your responsibility is to remain anchored in His word, not swayed by emotions or outside noise. Prayer must become a lifestyle, not a last resort. God-centered courtship means submitting decisions, boundaries, and expectations to Him consistently and together.

UNDERSTANDING COURTSHIP VS. DATING

Many people struggle in relationships because they confuse dating with courtship. These two approaches are not the same. Dating, as the world defines it, is often emotional exploration without commitment. It encourages people to follow feelings, test chemistry, move quickly, keep options open, and prioritize pleasure over purpose. Dating says, *"Let's see what happens."*

Courtship, on the other hand, says, *"Let's see what God says."*

Courtship is Christ-centered, has direction, and respect for God's timing. Rather than relying on emotion or trial and error, the focus is on preparing for a lifelong promise.

Dating tests people without purpose.

Courtship moves forward with prayer and spiritual understanding.

Dating follows emotions. Courtship follows God.

Dating seeks connection. Courtship seeks covenant.

My Personal Story: God's Confirmation in Courtship

My own courtship was shaped by faith, distance, and obedience. At the time, I lived in Puerto Rico, and he lived in New York. We had already built a strong friendship, and our romantic feelings grew naturally and prayerfully. But courtship required decisions that would impact our lives forever.

One of the confirmations I asked God for involved my grandmother. She raised me with strong values and was extremely protective. Growing up, she did not allow boys near our home. I remember a boy once stopping by, and she immediately sent him away, saying, *Yo no quiero porquería en mi casa*—"I don't want trash in my house." At the time, I was embarrassed. Years later, I realized God used her firmness to protect my heart.

So when I entered courtship with the man who would become my husband, I prayed,
"Lord, if this relationship is truly from You, let my grandmother accept him."

When he traveled to Puerto Rico to meet my family, I was nervous. But when he walked toward her and opened his arms to hug her, she hugged him back, warmly and without hesitation. He was the first and only man she ever welcomed into her home. At that moment, God confirmed what He had already spoken. This was one of several confirmations God revealed, affirming the direction He was leading me in.

WALKING IN PURITY DURING COURTSHIP

Purity is not old-fashioned.
Purity is protection.

Courtship deepens emotions and attraction, which is why boundaries are essential. Purity protects your spiritual clarity, your future marriage, and your testimony. Without boundaries, even strong believers can fall.

Purity requires intentional planning. Before temptation appears, boundaries must already be in place. For us, that meant avoiding passionate kissing, avoiding being alone in a private setting, and involving accountability when needed.

During our courtship, we found meaningful ways to spend time together while honoring those physical boundaries. My sister enjoyed every meal off the kids' menu whenever we went out to dinner. She did not realize it at the time, but God used her as our chaperone. Her presence helped us remain faithful to our commitment.

These were not rules imposed on us. They were boundaries we chose because we wanted God's blessing more than temporary pleasure. Romans 13:14 reminds us to "make no provision for the flesh."

If you have crossed boundaries, hear this with grace: God restores purity. Through repentance, you can reset and rebuild. Purity pursued today still honors God.

HANDLING CONFLICT DURING COURTSHIP

Conflict does not mean something is wrong, it often means growth is taking place.Healthy conflict builds empathy, protects emotional safety, and strengthens unity. Unhealthy conflict is marked by pride, personal attacks, and unresolved wounds. Courtship is a training ground for the communication you will one day carry into marriage. What you practice now becomes the foundation for covenant.

Just as physical boundaries matter, emotional boundaries set the dynamics for a healthy courtship that leads to a healthy marriage. Even when conflict arises, communication must remain effective, respectful, and rooted in love. Use words that clearly express your thoughts without causing harm, and be mindful of your tone and delivery. Respect must never be lost during disagreement. there should be no name-calling, aggressive tones, or emotional intimidation.

Avoid language that assigns blame or creates defensiveness, such as *"you always"* or *"you never."* Instead, focus on the issue at hand, not the person. This stage is an opportunity to learn one another, your communication styles, emotional needs, and how you each process conflict.

RESOLVING CONFLICT IN A HEALTHY WAY

Learning how to resolve conflict during courtship is essential, because the habits you form now will follow you into marriage. Scripture teaches us to be "quick to listen, slow to speak, and slow to become angry" (James 1:19). In courtship, this means learning to pause before reacting. It means choosing to listen fully, giving yourself space to pray, reflect, and respond with wisdom rather than emotion.

Healthy conflict during courtship focuses on addressing the issue, not attacking the person. The goal is understanding and resolution, not control or winning. One practical way to do this is by using "I" statements instead of accusations. For example, saying *"I feel unheard"* invites conversation, while *"You never listen"* creates defensiveness and shuts hearts down. How you speak matters just as much as what you say.

Communication must always be rooted in respect. There is no place for name-calling, sarcasm, or harsh language. Remember, you are speaking to God's son or God's daughter. God does not speak to His children with cruelty, and neither should you. Speak with clarity and love, and listen with humility, even when the conversation feels uncomfortable.

Conflict should never compromise emotional safety or lead to manipulation, intimidation, or pressure. If emotions escalate, it is wise to pause and revisit the conversation later. Pausing is not avoidance, it is maturity. It protects the heart and keeps the relationship healthy.

After the conflict is resolved, pray together. Inviting God into the process restores peace and strengthens unity. Learning to pray after disagreement during courtship builds a foundation for a marriage that knows how to fight *for* each other, not *against* each other.

When conflict is handled with humility, respect, and God at the center, it does not weaken the relationship, it prepares it.

One intentional practice we committed to during our courtship, and one that has continued to serve our marriage well, was taking the time to work through disagreements or misunderstandings before we ended our time together.

When we had disagreements, my man of God would often quote the famous Scripture from Ephesians 4:24 "Do not let the sun go down on your wrath"

I'll be honest, when he quoted that verse, it used to make my skin crawl. Not because it wasn't true, but because it forced me to face what I was feeling instead of avoiding it. And the Word of God *is* true, so I couldn't argue with it or justify He held tightly to that verse because, I will shut down meaning not talk, the reason for this was I carried baggage from my past and inside that baggage was do not trust and do not be vulnerable. Vulnerability felt like weakness, so I kept my walls up and my heart guarded. When he would gently ask, "What's wrong?" I would lie and say things like, "I'm just tired," or my famous line "It's my period." if you are a women reading this book, im sure you probably have use that line (LOL) But the truth was, i had a very hard time telling him I was hurt or upset about something he had done, and I didn't yet have the tools to express myself in a healthy way, instead i will not talk and treat him poorly with a attitude. But the Lord used at the time my boyfriend to expose me and he will express " "You're lying. The Holy Spirit just told me that's not true." That moment alone would undo me.

And still I will sit in silence, hoping eventually he would leave me alone. But he didn't. Not because he wanted to control me, but because he was on assignment to love me through my immature, and help me bring my voice out, looking back now as I am writing this book i asked myself why i was not able to tell him what bothered me, and i realize it was because i was afraid if i said something I will loose him,which was not true,

He would sit there patiently, gently asking, "What's wrong?" more than once. Not in anger. Not with pressure. But with persistence and care. He understood something I didn't yet understand: he was going to love me regarding what I was facing and that unresolved conflict doesn't disappear, it hides and grows and later on will damage our relationship.

We didn't wait until marriage to learn how to resolve conflict. We began practicing this during courtship. That discipline taught us how to confront issues, communicate honestly, and choose peace over pride. It wasn't easy. It was uncomfortable, but it laid a foundation that carried directly into our marriage.

Learning to resolve conflict shapes you into someone who listens with intention, speaks truth with love, remains present in discomfort, and chooses unity instead of running from tension. Courtship is not only about romance; it is where the foundation is built. It prepares you for how you will face conflict together, shaping your character, strengthening your bond, and preparing you for marriage.

Looking back, I am grateful we practiced this early. It taught me that love doesn't avoid hard conversations.
 Love leans in.
 Love stays.
 Love chooses resolution over silence, and grows stronger because of it.

RED FLAGS IN COURTSHIP
Warning Signs That Require Prayer and Discernment

While red flags in stage two, Friends in Love, often involve confusion or emotional instability, red flags in courtship are more serious. They usually point to issues of character, leadership, trust, and readiness for covenant.

Watch Carefully For The Following:

<u>Resistance to Spiritual Leadership or Accountability</u>
 A refusal to receive correction or submit to godly counsel is a warning sign of pride and immaturity.
 "Plans fail for lack of counsel, but with many advisers they succeed."
Proverbs 15:22

Pressure to Compromise Boundaries or Purity

Any pressure to cross physical, emotional, or spiritual boundaries reflects self-centered desire rather than covenant-minded love.

"For this is the will of God, your sanctification: that you should abstain from sexual immorality." 1 Thessalonians 4:3

Inconsistency Between Words and Actions

Integrity is revealed through consistency. When actions do not align with words, trust is weakened.

"The integrity of the upright guides them." Proverbs 11:3

Avoidance of Responsibility, Commitment, or Hard Conversations

Someone preparing for a covenant does not avoid responsibility or emotional depth.

"Whoever is faithful in little is also faithful in much." Luke 16:10

Lack of Trust or Excessive Secrecy

Extreme secrecy, such as refusing transparency in communication or guarding devices out of fear, undermines trust and emotional safety.

"For everything that is hidden will eventually be brought into the open." Luke 8:17

Dishonesty or Patterns of Lying

Truth is the foundation of covenant. Where dishonesty exists, trust cannot grow.

"The Lord detests lying lips, but He delights in people who are trustworthy." Proverbs 12:22

Controlling or Manipulative Behavior

Control is not love. Love honors freedom, dignity, and mutual respect.

"Love... does not insist on its own way." 1 Corinthians 13:5

Repeated Unresolved Conflict or Emotional Manipulation

When conflict is used to dominate, shame, or silence rather than restore, it damages unity and safety.

"Make every effort to live in peace with everyone." Romans 12:18

Red flags in courtship are not punishments, they are God's protection. They are not meant to create fear, but to invite wisdom. When something repeatedly disrupts peace, it requires prayerful attention and honest evaluation.

When two people come together in courtship, things naturally come to light. Courtship reveals patterns, character, and areas that may need growth. This is not automatically a sign to walk away. In many cases, red flags should first be prayed through together, discussed with humility, and brought before God with counsel.

Discernment also requires honesty. If concerning patterns continue even after prayer and counsel, and there is no real change, wisdom may call for letting go. Releasing at this stage is not unloving. It honors truth, protects both hearts, and acknowledges readiness.

Courtship is not the season to ignore warning signs in hopes that marriage will fix them. It is the season to lovingly discern whether both individuals are truly prepared to move toward covenant.

HOW TO NAVIGATE STAGE THREE: COURTSHIP

This stage requires maturity and intentional commitment, with God at the center rather than emotion or pressure.Scripture reminds us to trust God fully and surrender our own understanding to Him. When God leads, clarity replaces confusion, peace replaces pressure, and purpose becomes the foundation. (Proverbs 3:5–6).

Guard the relationship carefully, because courtship moves closer to covenant. What you nurture in this stage will shape your future marriage.Paying attention to small compromises, patterns, and attitudes protects what God is building.

Clear and honest communication becomes even more essential at this stage. Courtship requires the ability to address difficult topics with maturity and grace, speaking truth with love. Healthy communication builds trust, emotional safety, and unity. (Ephesians 4:15).

Boundaries must be firmly established and faithfully honored. As emotions and attraction deepen, purity and self-control protect spiritual clarity and future covenant. Scripture reminds us that not everything permissible is beneficial. Boundaries are not restrictions; they are protection. (1 Corinthians 10:23)

Do not walk this stage alone. Invite accountability and Godly counsel from trusted mentors, parents or spiritual leaders. Wise counsel brings clarity and perspective when emotions cloud discernment.(Proverbs 15:22).

Finally, move forward with discernment and peace rather than pressure or fear. God does not rush courtship. When peace remains, it confirms alignment. When peace consistently fades, it is an invitation to pause, pray, and seek God's direction.(Colossians 3:15).

PRAYER FOR STAGE 3:
COURTSHIP

Heavenly Father,
Thank You for guiding us into this sacred season. Teach us to honor You with our thoughts, decisions, and actions. Strengthen our boundaries, deepen our communication, and protect our hearts from temptation. Give us wisdom in moments of conflict, discernment in uncertainty, and peace in waiting. Keep our relationship rooted in purity, integrity, and spiritual unity. Lead us step by step toward the future You have prepared, and let everything we build bring glory to Your name.
In Jesus name, Amen.

Take time to sit with these questions in prayer:

1. How is God shaping me during this season of courtship?

2. What boundaries do we need to protect purity and emotional health?

3. How can we communicate in ways that reflect Christ more clearly?

4. Are we seeking God daily or relying on emotions?

5. What steps can we take now to strengthen the foundation for marriage?

STAGE 4: ENGAGEMENT

PREPARING FOR COVENANT

I CORINTHIANS 13:7 (NIV)

"IT ALWAYS PROTECTS, ALWAYS TRUSTS, ALWAYS HOPES, ALWAYS PERSEVERES.

STAGE 4: ENGAGEMENT
Preparing for Covenant

*E*ngagement is a joyful, sacred, and deeply transformative season.

If you have made it this far, pause and celebrate what God has done. What began as friendship grew into love, matured through courtship, and now, by the grace of God, you have a fiancé.
Look at God!

If you are single and reading ahead, this is still for you. Preparing your heart with wisdom now matters, no matter the season you are in.

Engagement is the moment two people say yes to each other and to the future God is calling them into. It is when intentions become clear and the relationship turns toward marriage. Engagement is more than excitement or wedding plans. It is not just preparing for a wedding...It is preparing for a covenant.

ENGAGEMENT IS MORE THAN PLANNING A WEDDING.

 It is the next and deeper level of courtship before marriage. This is the season when intentions are sealed and covenant is clearly in view. During engagement, God refines motives and strengthens unity while preparing both hearts for marriage. It is also often the enemy's final attempt to disrupt what God is establishing.

- When purpose is present, pressure follows.
- When a covenant draws near, unity becomes a target.

In the busyness of planning, it is easy to lose sight of God as stress and expectations take over. This is why engagement must be approached with prayer, humility, maturity, and spiritual discipline.

- Unity does not happen by accident. It must be protected and pursued.
- Unity is not the absence of conflict. It is the choice to remain connected through it.
- God builds unity.
- The enemy seeks to undermine it.

Scripture reminds us, *"Can two walk together unless they are agreed?"* (Amos 3:3). Two people cannot walk together unless they are in agreement. But agreement does not mean sameness; it means humility, communication, and a shared willingness to surrender to God and to one another. This becomes especially clear during engagement, when decisions like wedding venues and guest lists reveal how well two people navigate preferences, expectations, and compromise.

Strengthening unity during engagement requires intentional choices.

Strengthening unity during engagement requires intentional choices. It begins with learning to listen before speaking and choosing understanding over reaction.

It also means staying honest, even when conversations feel uncomfortable, and praying through disagreements rather than allowing them to create distance. Unity grows when love is chosen over pride and connection over control.

A couple united in spirit and anchored in prayer is difficult for the enemy to divide. When God remains at the center and unity is protected, engagement becomes more than preparation for marriage. It becomes a season of spiritual strengthening.

THE DAY HE PROPOSED

I will never forget the day my husband proposed to me, let me take you back to Sunday, March 11, 2002, my birthday. We were at our church in Manhattan, inside the beautiful United Palace. It was our fifth and final service of the day, and I was still wearing my dance ministry attire: a blue top, a flowing white ministry skirt, and freshly done bright red nails from the manicure and pedicure I had gotten the day before for my birthday celebration. I had just finished ministering on stage, and as I sat down afterward, still catching my breath and transitioning out of praise and worship, I was ready to hear my man of God share a testimony he had mentioned a week earlier. He had said, "Next Sunday, I'm going to share how I came to Christ and how my family followed." So I sat there prepared and expectant, ready to hear him testify about the goodness of God.

I was excited to hear him speak. He had told me parts of the story before, how he was the first one saved and how his mother, father, and sister eventually gave their lives to Jesus. I sat there ready to celebrate what God had done in his family... my soon to be family.

When he finished sharing, I heard my name "Thalia come up"

They called me to the stage.

I thought I was going up to share something too. I had no idea what was coming.

The moment I walked toward him, everything slowed down. He took my hand, and t in front of the entire congregation, he got on one knee.

My heart began beating so fast I thought everyone around me could hear it. The entire church stood up and began shouting, clapping, and rejoicing. But at that moment, I could barely hear the noise. It felt like time froze and the only voice I could hear was his.

He looked into my eyes and said the words my heart had been waiting for:

"Will you marry me?"

It was beautiful. Holy. Surreal. And of course, I said YES!

The church erupted in joy. Our pastors were celebrating, our families were overjoyed, and heaven was rejoicing with us. But let me tell you something: Heaven rejoiced, but hell did not.

Engagement is not just a romantic moment... It is a declaration of covenant. And the enemy hates covenant.

THE REALITY THAT FOLLOWED

After the excitement came the planning... and the warfare.
Our engagement season was filled with joy, but it also came with real challenges. This is not shared to scare you, but to prepare you. The enemy does not celebrate unity, purpose, or godly marriage. When God is forming something meaningful, opposition often follows.

During this season, the unity God was building was disrupted by pressure that showed up as stress, confusion, disagreements, outside voices, and fear.

I remember feeling overwhelmed at times. We were planning a wedding, searching for the right venue, preparing to move, and learning how to merge two lives into one. We had no guide, no roadmap, and no book like this one. We were figuring everything out as we went, navigating different personalities, opinions, and the reality of life changing so quickly.

There were moments when I didn't even feel I did not want to get married unlike courtship in where I had to learn to express my emotions during engagement. I had to learn how to deal with the pressure of preparing a wedding and building a home. At this stage we learned how to compromise with each other. If you are in this stage give each other grace not because we lacked love, but because the process felt heavy. We loved each other deeply, but the pressure for me was real.

We argued.
We disagreed.
We bumped heads.

We were learning how to become one while still unlearning old habits, fears, and expectations. On top of that, everyone had an opinion, friends, family, church members, and leaders. Their voices grew loud and, at times, overwhelming. But in the middle of it all, I remember hearing the Holy Spirit gently whisper to me: "Enjoy this season."

So we slowed down...
We prayed more...
We talked more...
We quieted outside voices...
We listened to each other's hearts...
We learned how to compromise...
We learned how to plan together...
And most importantly, we learned how to keep God at the center.

Because this is what engagement truly teaches you:
- You are not just planning a wedding.
- You are learning how to build a life.
- You are learning how to become one.

As we reflected on that season, we realized something important. What we experienced was not accidental. It was spiritual.

Engagement is not just a milestone; it is a threshold. It is the moment a relationship moves from intention to covenant, from promise to preparation. And whenever a covenant is approaching, spiritual opposition often follows. This is why it is important to understand what is happening beneath the surface during engagement.

Not because your relationship is wrong, but because it is right. The enemy does not waste time attacking what is weak. He targets what is anointed, purposeful, and aligned with God.

COVENANT ATTRACTS WARFARE.

As a relationship moves toward covenant, the enemy recognizes that a godly marriage is being formed, and that your future home will carry purpose, authority, and light. Because of that, he often attempts to interfere, not by attacking the relationship directly, but by working through:

- Doubt
- Insecurity
- Temptation
- Misunderstandings
- Unnecessary conflict
- Confusion
- Fear

Not because the relationship is wrong, but because God is building something meaningful.

Scripture reminds us, *"The thief comes only to steal and kill and destroy; I have come that they may have life, and have it abundantly"* (John 10:10).

Recognizing this helps you understand the nature of the battle without becoming consumed by it. The enemy does not waste time attacking what is weak. He targets what is anointed, purposeful, and aligned with God.

Understanding this keeps you from allowing the attack to create division between you or believing the lie that the problem is you or the relationship. Warfare during engagement is not always a sign that something is wrong. More often, it is a sign that something right is happening and a covenant is being established, something worth protecting, praying over, and standing firm for.

EMOTIONAL TRIGGERS DURING ENGAGEMENT

Along with spiritual warfare, another reality often rises during engagement: emotional triggers.

Engagement has a way of revealing what still needs healing. Because God loves you deeply, He often uses this season to bring to the surface areas that need His healing touch before a covenant is established. This does not mean healing is ever "finished." Healing is ongoing and continually surrendered to God, it does not stop at any stage.

Healing is not something you complete and mark on a check list and move on.. It is a lifelong journey of surrender, growth, and dependence on God.

Emotional triggers may surface in certain areas that friendship or courtship did not reveal. Marriage will reveal others as well. This does not mean you are failing or regressing,it means God is continuing His work in you. (Philippians 1:6).

During this season, God may gently bring things to the surface, insecurities, fears, unresolved heartbreak, rejection wounds, trust issues, abandonment triggers, emotional sensitivity, or fears of repeating unhealthy family patterns. These moments are not signs of weakness or failure. They are signs that God is preparing you. What rises in this stage, or in any stage, is not meant to shame you. It is meant to heal you.

As emotional triggers surface during engagement, they reveal an important truth: love alone is not enough to sustain a covenant, preparation is required. Awareness without tools can feel overwhelming, but God never reveals something without also providing a way to strengthen it. This is where premarital counseling becomes a gift.

PREMARITAL COUNSELING: A GIFT, NOT A BURDEN

As you approach covenant, it is important to consider premarital counseling. It is not a sign of weakness, but a wise and intentional step toward building a strong foundation for marriage. Premarital counseling helps prepare you for covenant by addressing areas that matter most *before* they become points of strain later.

Choosing premarital counseling does not mean something is wrong with your relationship. It means you are choosing to steward it wisely. It provides a safe, guided space to address emotional triggers, spiritual growth, communication patterns, and future expectations before they become sources of division.

Engaging in premarital counseling is an act of stewardship. It reflects a willingness to grow, to learn, and to build with intention rather than assumption. A strong covenant is not built by accident, it is built through preparation, humility, and wisdom.

Premarital counseling is not a sign of weakness.
It is wisdom. It is equally important to ensure that the person providing your premarital counseling aligns with your faith, values, and biblical convictions. The counselor, pastor, or mentor guiding

you should honor God's design for marriage, respect the authority of Scripture, and support the kind of covenant you are prayerfully preparing to build.

WHEN CHOOSING A PREMARITAL COUNSELOR, LOOK FOR SOMEONE WHO:

- Shares or respects your Christian faith and worldview
- Approaches marriage biblically, not just culturally or emotionally
- Encourages accountability, honesty, and spiritual growth
- Creates a safe space for difficult conversations without compromise
- Has wisdom, maturity, and experience walking couples toward covenant

Premarital counseling strengthens the very areas that covenant requires to thrive, including communication, conflict resolution, financial unity, emotional awareness, spiritual connection, healing, humility, and vision alignment. Scripture reminds us, *"Plans succeed with many advisers"* (Proverbs 15:22).

A successful marriage requires preparation, and premarital counseling is part of that preparation. It allows couples to engage in intentional, guided conversations that build understanding, alignment, and unity long before challenges arise. Rather than waiting for problems to surface, premarital counseling equips you to enter marriage informed, supported, and spiritually grounded, ready not just for a wedding day, but for a lifetime together.

Through Premarital Counseling, Couples are Given The Opportunity To Explore Important Areas Such As:

<u>Roles in Marriage</u>

You will discuss what the roles of husband and wife mean biblically—not culturally. This includes expectations around leadership, submission, teamwork, partnership, and mutual honor.

<u>Children</u>

You will talk through whether you desire children, how many, parenting styles, discipline, values, and the vision you share for raising a family.

<u>Finances</u>

You will address tithing, saving, spending, debt, budgeting, financial goals, and the importance of transparency and unity in stewardship.

<u>Faith Practices</u>

You will discuss prayer, church involvement, ministry, devotional life, and spiritual leadership within the home.

Family Boundaries

You will explore expectations around extended family, holidays, traditions, boundaries, and how to navigate conflict with wisdom and unity.

Communication Styles

You will learn how each person expresses emotions, processes conflict, and needs to feel heard, understood, and respected.

Purpose & Vision

You will clarify callings, dreams, long-term goals, and the kind of marriage and legacy you desire to build together.

These conversations are not meant to create fear or pressure. They are designed to prevent future conflict, deepen understanding, and build lifelong unity. Premarital counseling equips you to enter covenant informed, aligned, and spiritually grounded, ready not just for a wedding day, but for a lifetime together.

HOW TO NAVIGATE STAGE FOUR: ENGAGEMENT

The way you navigate stage 4, especially emotional triggers and spiritual warfare, should mirror how you have approached every stage of this journey: through prayer, fasting, and honest communication. The same spiritual disciplines that helped you discern the relationship are the ones that will sustain it as emotions rise and responsibilities increase.

Triggers are not an invitation to pull away from one another; they are an opportunity to grow closer. Engagement reveals how you respond under pressure—not just how you connect when everything feels easy. Learning to grow *through* emotional triggers, rather than away from each other, is part of building a healthy foundation for covenant.

This season requires openness and humility. Talk honestly about what is being triggered without blaming or accusing. Learn to listen with compassion rather than defensiveness. Validation does not mean agreement, it means acknowledging the other person's experience and honoring their vulnerability.

Bring emotional wounds before God together. Pray over past pain, fears, and insecurities. Ask the Holy Spirit to bring clarity, healing, and truth. Allow Him to reveal what belongs to the past and what requires wisdom in the present. Healing happens when light is invited into wounded places.

Patience is essential in this stage. Emotional growth does not happen overnight. Some areas require time, consistency, and grace.

Be willing to extend the same patience to one another that God continually extends to you.

Above all, ask the Holy Spirit for wisdom. He knows what is surfacing and why. He guides, comforts, convicts, and heals with perfect understanding. When you submit your emotions to Him, He teaches you how to love well, respond wisely, and walk in unity.

Covenant requires emotional health, and engagement is where that foundation is strengthened—not by avoiding difficult moments, but by facing them together with God at the center.

And yes—enjoy this season.

If you are a woman, try on as many wedding dresses as you can. Let yourself laugh, dream, and celebrate what God is doing.
 If you are a man, enjoy the process too, try on the tuxes, imagine the day, and take pride in preparing for your future.

Joy is not a distraction from holiness; it is part of it. Scripture reminds us, *"There is a time to weep and a time to laugh... a time to mourn and a time to dance"* (Ecclesiastes 3:4).

Engagement is a sacred season, but it is also a joyful one. Let God shape you, heal you, and prepare you... and don't forget to celebrate along the way.

RED FLAGS DURING ENGAGEMENT

Engagement is a season of preparation, not pressure. While challenges are normal, there are certain warning signs that should not be ignored. Red flags during engagement often point to deeper issues that require prayerful attention, wise counsel, and honest evaluation *before* marriage is established.

Red flags are not meant to create fear or suspicion. They are invitations to pause, seek God, and respond with wisdom. Engagement is the final season before covenant, what is consistently present now will not disappear after the wedding.

Watch For The Following:

Resistance to Premarital Counseling or Accountability

A refusal to receive guidance, correction, or biblical counsel may indicate pride or emotional immaturity.

"Plans fail for lack of counsel, but with many advisers they succeed." (Proverbs 15:22)

Pressure to Rush the Process

Healthy preparation allows room for discernment. Urgency driven by fear, lust, or control is a warning sign.

"The plans of the diligent lead surely to abundance." (Prov 21:5)

Chronic Conflict Without Resolution

Disagreements are normal, but unresolved conflict that repeats without growth or repentance signals deeper issues. *"Do not let the sun go down while you are still angry."* (Ephesians 4:26)

Dishonesty or Lack of Transparency

Trust is foundational to covenant. Patterns of lying, withholding truth, or secrecy—especially around communication, finances, or boundaries—undermine unity. *"The Lord detests lying lips, but He delights in people who are trustworthy."* (Proverbs 12:22)

Controlling or Manipulative Behavior

Control is rooted in fear, not love. Covenant requires mutual honor, freedom, and respect.

"Love... does not insist on its own way." (1 Corinthians 13:5)

Spiritual Imbalance or Avoidance

A lack of spiritual leadership, inconsistency in faith, or avoidance of prayer and Scripture can weaken the foundation of covenant.

"Can two walk together unless they are agreed?" (Amos 3:3)

Persistent Loss of Peace

If peace is continually disrupted and replaced with anxiety, confusion, or dread, it is an invitation to pause and seek God's direction. *"Let the peace of Christ rule in your hearts."* (Colossians 3:15). Red flags during engagement are not accusations—they are indicators. They do not mean you have failed or chosen wrongly, but they do require honesty, prayer, and discernment. Engagement is not the season to hope issues will resolve themselves after marriage. It is the season to address them with wisdom, humility, and courage. Covenant is too sacred to build on unresolved warning signs.

PRAYER FOR STAGE 4: ENGAGEMENT

Father, Thank You for guiding us to this sacred season of preparation. As we move toward covenant, align our hearts with Your will. Protect our relationship from every spiritual attack, every distraction, and every plan of the enemy.Strengthen our unity. Deepen our communication.Purify our intentions. Heal anything in us that is not ready for marriage. Give us wisdom, patience, and discernment. Teach us how to love like Christ, with humility, gentleness, forgiveness, and honor. Prepare us for a marriage that reflects Your heart.

Cover our engagement, our families, our decisions, and our future home. Lead us step by step into the covenant You have ordained. In Jesus' name, Amen.

<u>**REFLECTION QUESTIONS**</u>

Take time to sit with these questions in prayer:

1. What emotional areas is God bringing to the surface for healing?

2. How can you deepen unity with your fiancé in this season?

3. What boundaries do you need to strengthen to protect purity and peace?

4. What expectations do you still need to discuss together?

5. Are there any warning signs God is asking you to pay attention to?

6. How can you prioritize spiritual preparation over wedding preparation?

STAGE 5: MARRIAGE

GOD'S DESIGN

1 CORINTHIANS 13:7 (NIV)

"IT ALWAYS PROTECTS, ALWAYS TRUSTS, ALWAYS HOPES, ALWAYS PERSEVERES

Let All Things be done decently & in order
1 Cor 14:40

STAGE 5: MARRIAGE
God's Design

What began as friendship grew into love, matured through courtship, was sealed through engagement, and now, by the grace of God, has entered the sacred covenant of marriage.

Whether you are already married, currently planning a wedding, or simply reading ahead, I want you to pause here with me. This stage is one of my favorites, not because it is easy, but because it is sacred. Marriage is God's idea. It was not created by culture, trends, or tradition. It was not designed by society or shaped by the times. Marriage was created by God Himself, and everything He creates is good. This is the sacred stage where two become one under His hand. It is where covenant is formed, purpose is aligned, and love is refined through His design and grace.

Marriage becomes the lifelong classroom of the Holy Spirit. It is where God takes two individuals and forms one unified covenant. The Bible tells us that "the two shall become one," and I often smile when I think about that verse, because when I got married, I truly believed that the moment we said *"I do,"* everything would instantly fall into perfect unity. God definitely has a sense of humor. No one told me that becoming one is a process. It sounds beautiful and it is, but it is also work.

When you say *"I do,"* you become one by covenant. But learning how to walk in that oneness takes time. through submission to

God, walking in agreement, building strong communication, and forgiveness.

Oneness is real the moment you say *"I do,"* but learning how to walk in that oneness is a lifelong process. You are one by covenant, yet you must learn how to live as one, how to think together, decide together, forgive together, and submit to God together. And yes, you will notice the word *together* repeated often, because marriage is lived that way. You build a life together. You raise children together. You build a business together You buy a home together. You face challenges together. Marriage teaches you how to work and grow in unity with God at the center.

Oneness is established at the altar.
Agreement is developed over time.

Learning how to walk in unity, especially when you see things differently, is part of becoming one. And when God remains at the center, unity is not forced; it is formed.

REFINEMENT: HOW TWO BECOME ONE
So how do two people actually become one?

The answer is simple, but the process is not. Becoming one requires refinement.

Refinement looks much like the process used to purify gold. Raw gold does not begin shiny or beautiful. It must first be crushed and washed. Then it is placed into intense heat, not to destroy it, but to purify it. As the gold melts, impurities rise to the surface, and the refiner carefully removes them. This does not happen once. It happens again and again until the gold becomes pure. The fire is never meant to ruin the gold; it is meant to cleanse it and make it better.

In the same way, God uses marriage to refine us. He allows pressure, differences, and challenges to surface, not to harm us, but to reveal what needs healing. Pride, selfishness, fear, and old wounds rise to the surface so they can be addressed and removed. Over time, as we submit to the process, God's reflection becomes visible in how we love, forgive, and walk together as one.

Becoming one is hard work. It requires dedication, humility, patience, forgiveness, and perseverance. It means walking through uncomfortable moments, learning how to yield, and choosing love even when it costs you something. I often tell people, *"If you want to be more like Jesus, get married."* Jesus loved sacrificially. He forgave repeatedly. He chose love even when He was betrayed. Marriage invites us to do the same, daily, intentionally, and with grace.

Marriage is not about perfection. It is about refinement.

In the process of becoming one, God will teach you how to love like Christ—with patience, sacrifice, humility, and grace. He will reveal areas that need healing so you can love from wholeness, not wounds. He will sharpen your character, forming forgiveness and selflessness within you. He will deepen your spiritual life as you and your spouse learn how to pray, worship, and seek Him together. He will align your purpose, calling you into unity and kingdom assignment. He will strengthen your unity, making your home a fortress the enemy cannot easily divide. And He will build legacy, because marriage is not just about the present; it is about generations to come.

When God said, "The two shall become one flesh" (Genesis 2:24), He was not describing a moment, He was describing a process. Becoming one is not instant...it takes time. And remember this: God does not use the fire to shame you or break you. He uses it to transform you.

MARRIAGE IS A COVENANT, NOT MERELY A CONTRACT

Now that you understand refinement, you must also understand what you are truly committing to. To understand marriage correctly, we must understand the difference between a contract and a covenant.

Marriage may be recognized legally as a contract, but biblically it was never meant to be lived as one. Scripture reminds us that marriage is a covenant witnessed by God Himself (Malachi 2:14).

A contract is a legal agreement based on mutual benefit. It focuses on terms and conditions, protects individual interests, and can be dissolved when one party fails to uphold their part. A contract is upheld by law, not by love. It says, "If you do your part, I'll do mine. If you fail, I leave."

Marriage, however, is entered spiritually as a covenant.

A covenant is sacred and spiritual. It is rooted in commitment, not convenience. It is upheld by God, not just people. A covenant is sealed by promise, not performance. It says, "Even when it's hard, I stay, not because of emotion, but because of the vow I made before God."

When Jesus spoke of marriage, He did not describe a flexible arrangement. He declared permanence: *"What God has joined together, let no one separate."* (Mark 10:9).

Contracts may change when feelings change.
Covenants remain even when feelings shift.

Contracts protect rights.
Covenants lay them down.

Contracts rely on human strength.
Covenants are sustained by God's grace.

A contract says, *"I will stay as long as this benefits me."*
A covenant says, *"I give myself fully to you before God—permanently."*

Marriage will teach you more about yourself than any other relationship. Let me be completely honest, the refining process can hurt. It stretches, confronts and humbles you. But it is worth every moment. When God allows fire in your marriage, it is never to destroy you. It is always to refine you, shaping you more fully into His image

Scripture tells us, *"As iron sharpens iron, so one person sharpens another."* Proverbs 27:17

Iron sharpening iron is not soft or gentle. It creates pressure, sparks, and heat. That sharpening happens through friction, and friction simply means two things rubbing against each other. In marriage, friction occurs when two different people, with different backgrounds, personalities, habits, expectations, and wounds, come together in real life. That rubbing creates tension, not to break the marriage, but to reveal what needs growth.

Under God's hand, friction becomes a tool. It shapes your character, strengthens your union, and refines your love.

In the same way, marriage applies pressure to areas that need maturity, friction to areas that need smoothing, and heat to places in your heart that still need healing. Just as a jeweler refines gold, God uses the covenant of marriage to purify what is within you. Raw gold is unpolished and mixed with impurities. When exposed to fire, the gold melts and the impurities rise to the surface. The refiner carefully removes them, knowing the fire is never meant to destroy the gold, only to beautify it. That is what God does through marriage.

Marriage is not just a relationship; it is a sacred, lifelong covenant before God. Jesus affirmed this when He said,
"What God has joined together, let no one separate." Mark 10:9

In God's eyes, marriage is holy.
In God's eyes, marriage is binding.
In God's eyes, marriage carries eternal purpose

GOD'S PURPOSE FOR MARRIAGE

Marriage carries divine purpose. It is not an accident, not a cultural invention, and not merely an emotional connection between two people. Marriage was birthed in the heart and mind of God before sin ever entered the world. Because of that, it carries weight, glory, and eternal intention.

What God designs always has purpose, and marriage is no exception. It is sacred, intentional, and deeply spiritual. When God joins two people together, He is not only uniting hearts; He is establishing a covenant with meaning far beyond the wedding day.

Partnership — Walking in Agreement Under God's Direction

Marriage is not two people dragging each other through life. It is two people choosing to walk side by side, aligned in purpose, vision, and spiritual direction. Scripture asks, *"Can two walk together, unless they are agreed?"* (Amos 3:3)

Agreement does not mean perfection or sameness. It means choosing unity even when opinions differ. It means committing to peace, alignment, and the direction God is leading, together. A godly marriage is a partnership where you build together, pray together, dream together, and grow together. You are not competitors. You are companions on purpose.

Fruitfulness — Producing Life, Legacy, and Kingdom Impact

Fruitfulness in marriage is more than having children, though children are a blessing. Fruitfulness means producing God-honoring results through your union. God's first instruction to marriage was, *"Be fruitful and multiply"* (Genesis 1:28).

Your marriage is meant to produce spiritual fruit, emotional maturity, ministry impact, generational blessing, wise stewardship, and kingdom influence. A marriage under God's hand becomes a seed that continues producing long after your lifetime. What you build together echoes into generations.

Protection — Covering, Strength, and Spiritual Support

One of the most overlooked purposes of marriage is protection. *"Two are better than one... If either of them falls, one can help the other up"* (Ecclesiastes 4:9–12).

Marriage provides emotional covering, spiritual support, accountability, strength in weakness, and protection during warfare. The enemy loves isolation because isolation creates vulnerability. But unity creates strength. A husband and wife walking in agreement become a fortress the enemy cannot easily penetrate.

Spiritual Growth — Becoming More Like Christ

Marriage is one of God's most powerful tools for sanctification. Living closely with another person exposes pride, impatience, selfishness, wounds, and blind spots. But it also reveals your capacity to love deeply, forgive freely, sacrifice willingly, and walk in humility. Marriage holds up a mirror and invites you to choose Christ's character daily. God uses marriage not to punish you, but to refine you—to stretch you, mature you, and transform you into His likeness.

Reflecting Christ and the Church — A Living Gospel

Marriage is a prophetic picture of Christ's covenant with His bride, the Church. *"Husbands, love your wives, just as Christ loved the church..."* (Ephesians 5:25–32)

Your marriage preaches a sermon without words. Every act of forgiveness, patience, tenderness, sacrifice, and faithfulness reflects the gospel. A godly marriage shows the world what covenant looks like, what sacrificial love looks like, what unity looks like, and what grace looks like.

Marriage is not just companionship. It is a divine assignment—one designed to reveal God's heart to the world.

CONSECRATING THE MARRIAGE

A Prayer to Begin Your Marriage Covenant
On the night of our honeymoon, before anything else, we paused.
We held hands and we prayed.

Before intimacy, before rest, before celebration—we chose to
acknowledge God and invite Him fully into our marriage. I want
to encourage you to do the same. Whether it is the night of your
honeymoon, your first night in your home, or a quiet moment
soon after your wedding, take time to pause and pray together.
This moment is not about perfection. It is about intention.
Marriage begins best when it begins with God at the center.
That night, we made a covenant before the Lord and with each
other.

We prayed and declared:
"Lord, You are the center of our marriage.
We choose covenant, not convenience.
We commit to honor You and each other in every season."

Then we each prayed individually.

Husband's Prayer
"Lord, every part of me belongs to You and to my wife. My body,
my thoughts, my desires, my eyes, my lips—
all are reserved for the woman You have given me. No other
woman will have access to what belongs to my wife alone. I choose
faithfulness, purity, and honor."

Wife's Prayer
"Lord, every part of me belongs to You and to my husband.
My body, my heart, my desires, my affection—
all are reserved for the man You have given me.
No other man will have access to what belongs to my husband
alone. I choose faithfulness, purity, and honor."

That moment marked the difference between a contract and a
covenant. We did not rush into intimacy. We rushed into
commitment before God.

A covenant is not upheld by emotion. It is upheld by choice.
It is sustained by prayer. And it is protected through daily
surrender.

I encourage you to create your own sacred moment like this. Speak
it out loud. Pray together. Invite God into the foundation of your
marriage. What you consecrate to Him at the beginning, He is
faithful to protect in every season that follows.

WHERE THERE IS COVENANT, THERE WILL BE WARFARE

Marriage is God's design, and that is exactly why the enemy fights
it so fiercely. Anything God creates to carry purpose, unity, and
legacy becomes a target. Covenant is not just a romantic agreement
between two people; it is a spiritual union established by God
Himself.

And wherever God establishes a covenant, the enemy attempts interference.

The enemy does not hate marriage because it is difficult. He hates marriage because it is powerful. He hates what marriage represents. Marriage represents:

- unity
- agreement
- godly families
- spiritual authority
- generational blessing
- legacy
- purpose

Marriage reflects Christ and the Church. It preaches the gospel without words; And because of that, the enemy's goal has always been the same: divide what God has joined.

Scripture reminds us: "For we do not wrestle against flesh and blood, but against principalities, against powers, against the rulers of the darkness of this age…" (Ephesians 6:12)

This means your greatest battles in marriage are rarely about the surface issue. They are spiritual at the root.

THE STRATEGY OF THE ENEMY: DIVISION

One of the enemy's oldest and most effective tactics is division. He does not usually attack marriages head-on. Instead, he works subtly, patiently, and strategically. He looks for cracks, wounds, exhaustion, unhealed places, and moments of vulnerability.

He attacks through miscommunication, offense, unspokenness, unmet expectations, temptations, outside voices, comparison, old wounds, pride, assumptions, fatigue and burnout.

His goal is simple. It is to get you to turn against each other instead of towards each other. That is why Scripture warns us: "Do not give the devil a foothold." (Ephesians 4:27)
A foothold may be small, but if ignored, it grows.

YOUR SPOUSE IS NOT YOUR ENEMY

Because marriage is made in God's image and it has a divine assignment, one designed to reveal God's heart to the world. It's important to be aware of the enemy of your soul

One of the enemy's biggest tactics in marriage is convincing you that your spouse is the problem. He whispers lies to make you believe your fight is against your spouse, when in reality, your spouse is not your enemy.

Now let's be clear, not everything is the devil. Sometimes we are simply human, which means we can make poor decisions, react out of immaturity, let the flesh lead, etc. The Bible warns us about the lust of the flesh, the lust of the eyes, and the pride of life. So we must stay honest and take responsibility.

But hear me clearly: the enemy's mission is division. He wants to turn covenant into competition. He wants to make you fight each other instead of fighting for each other.

RECOGNIZING THE VOICES IN YOUR MARRIAGE

One of the most important skills in marriage is learning to recognize which voice is speaking in moments of conflict.
There are only three voices you will ever encounter:

1. God's voice
2. The enemy's voice
3. Your own voice

HOW DO YOU KNOW WHICH VOICE IS SPEAKING?

- If it aligns with Scripture , then it's God's voice. God's voice brings peace, conviction, wisdom, clarity, and unity.

- If it produces fear, division, accusation, confusion, or shame, then it's the enemy's voice. Satan is the accuser, he whispers lies designed to separate what God has joined together.

- If it is emotional, reactive, or rooted in past wounds, then it's your own voice. Our human voice often speaks from pain, insecurity, or unhealed areas.

In the heat of emotion, they may sound similar. But the more you grow spiritually, the easier it becomes to distinguish them.

Jesus said, *"My sheep know My voice."* (John 10:27).
The more you walk with God, the more His voice becomes familiar and steady.

God's voice leads you toward unity. The enemy's voice pushes you toward division. Your own voice fluctuates with your emotions.

You'd be surprised how often we speak with married couples and hear the *exact same lies*:

- "Your spouse doesn't care."
- "You are better off alone."
- "You married the wrong person."
- "They don't love you anymore."
- "They're your enemy, not your partner."

None of those lies are new.
None of them come from God.
And none of them align with His Word.

RESOLVING CONFLICT IN MARRIAGE
Fighting *For* Unity, Not Against Each Other

Conflict in marriage is inevitable. Two different people, with different backgrounds, personalities, communication styles, and expectations, are learning how to live as one. Disagreement does not mean your marriage is failing, but division is never God's design.

In a covenant, the goal is never to win an argument. The goal is to protect unity.

Healthy marriages, remember, I said healthy, not perfect. Perfect marriages do not exist, but healthy ones do. One of the ways to cultivate a healthy marriage is learning how to fight fair—not by avoiding conflict, but by handling it with wisdom, humility, and love. Biblical truth, along with years of marital wisdom, confirms this: connection, not competition, is the key to navigating conflict. Marriage becomes damaging when spouses turn against each other instead of turning toward one another.

Scripture reminds us, *"Be quick to listen, slow to speak, and slow to become angry"* (James 1:19). Godly conflict begins with posture, not posture toward each other, but posture before God.

Slow The Moment Down

When emotions rise, resist the urge to react immediately. Pause. Breathe. Pray. A delayed response rooted in wisdom is far more powerful than an instant reaction fueled by emotion. Slowing the moment allows the Holy Spirit to lead the conversation instead of emotion.

Address The Issue, Not The Identity

Conflict should never attack who your spouse is. Focus on the issue, not the person. Speak from your own experience rather than accusation. Saying, *"I felt hurt,"* invites understanding, while *"you always"* or *"you never"* invites defense. The goal is resolution—not control.

Communicate With Honor and Respect

Words create an atmosphere. Tone communicates value. Remember, you are speaking to someone created in the image of God. Name-calling, sarcasm, belittling language, or verbal aggression tear down emotional safety and weaken trust. Truth spoken without love wounds; love spoken without truth avoids. A healthy marriage requires both.

Stay Present—Don't Withdraw

Silence, shutdown, and emotional withdrawal may feel safer than engagement, but unresolved conflict does not disappear—it hides and grows. Staying emotionally present communicates commitment. It says, *"I'm here. We matter. This is worth working through."*

Honor Boundaries During Conflict

Conflict should never compromise emotional, spiritual, or physical safety. If emotions escalate, it is wise to take a break—but always with the intention to return and restore. Walking away to calm

down is healthy; walking away to avoid the issue is harmful.
Boundaries protect the covenant.

Pray Together After Resolution

Inviting God into the moment restores peace and re-centers the marriage. Prayer softens hearts, humbles pride, and reminds both spouses that the covenant is bigger than the conflict. When God is welcomed into disagreement, unity is strengthened. When conflict is handled with maturity and grace, it becomes a place of growth instead of division. It teaches you to listen with intention, speak truth with love, sit in discomfort without withdrawing, and choose unity over ego. These moments shape the character of your marriage.

Marriage does not thrive because conflict never happens.
Marriage thrives because conflict is handled with love.

At Its core, Fighting For Unity Looks Like This:

You attack the problem, not each other.
You remind yourselves, *"We are on the same team."*
You pause before reacting and allow emotions to settle.
You seek understanding before defending your position.
You ask, *"Help me understand what you meant."*
You pray together instead of pulling apart.
You refuse to threaten divorce, because safety strengthens connection.

You choose restoration over winning—because winning an argument but losing connection is never victory.

GUARDRAILS THAT PROTECT THE COVENANT

Every marriage needs protection. Love alone is not enough, guardrails keep the marriage safe when emotions run high and pressure comes. These guardrails are not rules meant to restrict love; they are protections designed to preserve it.

I want to share one powerful commitment my husband and I made early, during Stage 4, our engagement, and reaffirmed on the night of our wedding. This commitment has sustained our marriage as the writing of this book for 22 years.

Guardrail One: The "D-Word" Does Not Exist

We made a covenant before God that we would never speak the word "divorce." We call it *the D-word*, and it does not exist in our home. We don't say it. We don't threaten it. And we don't practice it. That does not mean the thought never crossed my mind, especially in moments of anger or frustration. But I never allowed it to come out of my mouth. Every time the thought tried to rise, the Holy Spirit would remind me of the covenant we made before God. Words carry power. What you allow into your vocabulary eventually finds its way into your behavior.

What does it mean to not practice divorce?

It means we do not rehearse separation while claiming a covenant. The Bible teaches us, *"Do not let the sun go down on your wrath."* (Ephesians 4:26). Now, in marriage, this can look different. Sometimes you need a pause. Sometimes you need rest. Sometimes you need to sleep it off. But we stayed in the same bed. We did not use distance as punishment.

<u>Not practicing divorce means:</u>
- We do not sleep in separate beds
- We do not move out or go stay with family or friends
- We do not remove our wedding rings
- We do not threaten separation during conflict

Why? Because the enemy's mission is division. And we refused to give him access.

If you are married, I encourage you to make this commitment before God together. And if the D-word has been spoken or practiced in your marriage, there is grace. Repent together. Recommit together. And remove it from your covenant language.

<u>Guardrail Two: Words Must Build, Not Break</u>

We also committed to never cursing or disrespecting one another with our words. No name-calling. No belittling. No verbal attacks. Words are meant to build up, not tear down.

In heated moments, wisdom says pause. Early in our marriage, we practiced what we called the "time-out method." If one of us felt overwhelmed or angry, we would say, "Time out." The conversation stopped; not to avoid the issue, but to calm our hearts.

Sometimes that meant stepping away to pray. Sometimes it meant repenting before God individually. But we always returned to the conversation with humility and clarity.

<u>Guardrail Three: Protect the Marriage From Outside Voices</u>
We made a firm commitment to never bash our spouse—to anyone, especially to the opposite sex. Your spouse's weaknesses are not public information. Marriage thrives in honor and discretion, not exposure.

<u>Guardrail Four: No Private Access to the Opposite Sex</u>
Another guardrail we established was transparency with communication. Private messages, calls, or texts with the opposite sex were not acceptable. If a woman needed to reach my husband, I was included. If a man needed to reach me, my husband was included. This removed secrecy and gave no room for the enemy.

<u>Guardrail Five: Radical Honesty About Temptation</u>
Finally, we committed to honesty, even about temptation. If either of us felt tempted, noticed inappropriate attention, or sensed a boundary being tested, we brought it into the light immediately. Sin grows in darkness, but freedom grows in the light. I told my husband when someone flirted with me in a store. He's told me when situations felt uncomfortable at work. And instead of shame, we prayed. That level of honesty builds deep trust and spiritual safety. These guardrails are not about control, they are about covering. They have protected our covenant, strengthened our unity, and kept our marriage aligned with God's heart. Where a

covenant is honored, grace multiplies. Where guardrails are in place, love remains protected.

INVESTING IN YOUR MARRIAGE

Remember, it is essential to invest in your marriage. A healthy, thriving marriage does not grow by accident , it grows through intentional effort. Just like your walk with God requires consistency, devotion, and time, your marriage also needs continual nourishment.

Think back to Stage 2 and Stage 3, when you were falling in love. You made time for each other. You talked for hours. You were curious, attentive, and emotionally present. That investment helped your relationship grow in the early stages, and the same is required now.

Marriage doesn't automatically stay strong just because you said "I do."
You must continue finding ways to pursue God and each other. Your covenant needs consistent attention, affection, and care.

One of the greatest gifts you can give your relationship is a shared commitment to grow, spiritually, emotionally, and relationally. Marriage is a living covenant; it must be fed, nurtured, and strengthened regularly.

If you neglect a garden, weeds will take over.
If you neglect a fire, it burns out.
If you neglect a marriage, distance begins to form.

But when you invest in it, when you water it, protect it, and prioritize it, your marriage becomes fruitful, resilient, and life-giving. It produces the kind of love that lasts through every stage of life.

So how do you invest in your marriage in a practical, intentional way?

Here Are Simple and Powerful, Ways To Strengthen Your Connection & Keep Your Covenant Thriving:

Attend Marriage Retreats

One powerful way to invest in your marriage is by attending marriage conferences and retreats. These spaces are not just events on a calendar, they are intentional moments set apart to realign your hearts with God and with each other.

Marriage conferences create room to pause, step away from daily responsibilities, and focus on what truly matters. Life moves fast. Work, children, ministry, finances, and responsibilities can slowly pull couples into survival mode. Conferences interrupt that cycle. They give you space to breathe, reflect, and hear God's voice clearly again, both individually and together. Be on the look out for a Love in order conference.

In these settings, God often brings clarity, healing, and renewed vision. You hear teaching that speaks directly to areas you didn't even realize needed attention. Sometimes God confirms what He has already been whispering to your heart. Other times, He gently exposes patterns that need to be addressed before they cause deeper wounds.

What makes conferences especially powerful is that they remind you that you are not alone. You see other couples — in different seasons, with different stories — all choosing to invest in their covenant. That kind of environment strengthens hope and normalizes the work it takes to build a healthy marriage. It breaks the lie that "we're the only ones struggling" or "something must be wrong with us."

Retreats and conferences also provide opportunities to reconnect emotionally and spiritually. They create moments for prayer together, honest conversation, laughter, and reflection. Many couples walk away refreshed, refocused, and re-centered on God's purpose for their marriage.

Marriage grows when it is intentionally nourished. When you choose to step away, lean in, and seek God together, He honors that posture. What you invest in your marriage today becomes the strength that carries you through tomorrow.

Join Marriage Connect Groups or Small Groups

Marriage was never meant to be lived in isolation. God designed a covenant to grow in community. When couples are surrounded by godly support, strength, wisdom, and encouragement increase. Marriage connect groups create space to learn, grow, and walk alongside other couples who are also committed to honoring God. These groups remind you that you are not alone in the journey and that growth is normal. Through shared experiences, prayer, and accountability, marriages are strengthened and sharpened.

Scripture tells us, "As iron sharpens iron, so one person sharpens another." (Proverbs 27:17). God uses community to protect, encourage, and strengthen covenant. Investing in godly relationships around your marriage helps guard unity and provides support in every season.

Engage in Marriage Counseling When Needed

Seeking counseling is not a sign of weakness; it is a sign of wisdom and maturity. Spirit-filled counseling provides a safe space to heal past wounds, improve communication, break unhealthy patterns, and rebuild trust and intimacy.

Some of the strongest marriages are not those that avoided help, but those that were humble enough to seek it. Choosing guidance is choosing growth. It is an act of stewardship over the covenant God has entrusted to you.

Go on Dates — Keep Pursuing Each Other

Dating should not stop once you get married. It is one of the simplest and most powerful ways to maintain connection, joy, and intimacy. You don't need luxury or grand plans — you need intention.

Dates create space to talk without distraction, laugh together, nurture romance, and keep friendship alive. They allow you to reconnect emotionally and physically, reminding each other why you chose one another.

Marriage grows when friendship is continually nurtured. Never stop pursuing each other. Never stop dating. Never stop enjoying the gift God gave you in one another.

Your Marriage Is Worth the Investment

Everything beautiful requires care. Your marriage is a garden and intentional investment keeps it flourishing.

The more you pour into your marriage, the more God will pour out His peace, unity, joy, and strength.

THE GIFT OF GODLY COMMUNITY IN MARRIAGE

One of the most meaningful details of a wedding day that is often overlooked is the bridal party. Bridesmaids and groomsmen are not just there for photographs or tradition. Their presence carries purpose.

They stand beside you on your wedding day as a reminder: you were never meant to do marriage alone.

As you step into a covenant, God does not call you into isolation. He surrounds you with community; with brothers and sisters in Christ who will walk with you through seasons of joy, transition, and hardship.

For women, it is vital to keep godly girlfriends close. You will need them. You will need sisters who can pray with you, encourage you, speak truth, and walk beside you in the many seasons marriage brings: pregnancy, childbirth, parenting, health challenges, celebrations, and moments when your emotions feel heavy.

I remember when I was pregnant and my husband was working. One of my sisters in Christ would go with me to my doctor's appointments. Later, after giving birth, I struggled with postpartum depression. My sisters were there to clean my home, cook meals, and support me in ways only a godly community can. They were instruments of God's care in a vulnerable season of my life.

In the same way, men need godly brothers. My husband needed men who could pray with him, stand with him, and support him; especially during difficult seasons, like when his father was diagnosed with dementia. He needed brothers who could help him carry emotional weight, intercede with him, and remind him of God's faithfulness.

This is why godly friendships remain important even after marriage.

Marriage does not replace community—it is strengthened by it.

Of course, boundaries and discernment are essential. Community must always honor the covenant. But isolation is not God's design. Scripture reminds us that two are better than one, and that principle extends beyond marriage into godly fellowship.

God will send the right sisters and the right brothers to walk alongside you and your spouse. These relationships help keep you grounded, supported, and spiritually covered.

That is why a bridal party exists. Not just to celebrate with you, but to remind you that you will need one another.

Marriage flourishes when a covenant is supported by the community.

PRAYER FOR STAGE 5:
MARRIAGE

Lord, We present our marriage before You.
Thank You for joining us in covenant.
Teach us to love with patience, compassion, and humility.
Protect our home from division and spiritual attacks.
Make us quick to forgive, slow to anger, and eager to serve one another.

Strengthen our communication, intimacy, and unity.
Help us build a legacy that honors You for generations.
Lead us, guide us, and keep us rooted in Your presence.
In Jesus name,
Amen.

Take time to sit with these questions in prayer:

1. How can we keep God at the center of our marriage on a daily basis — not just during difficult moments, but in our everyday routines?

2. What areas of our communication need strengthening, and what new habits can we build to create emotional safety for each other?

3. Are there any unresolved wounds, offenses, or emotional triggers that need forgiveness or healing? How can we address them with grace and humility?

4. What steps can we take to protect unity in our home, especially during moments of conflict or spiritual pressure

5. Are we fully committed to removing the D-word (divorce) from our relationship and walking in covenant, not contract? How can we reinforce that commitment?

6. How can we invest more intentionally in our marriage — through date nights, retreats, counseling, shared learning, or quality time?

7. What spiritual practices do we want to build together (prayer, fasting, daily devotion, worship), and how can we make them consistent?

8. What lies or negative thoughts have we believed about each other, and how can we replace them with God's truth?

9. How can we better honor, support, and serve each other as we grow in oneness?

TIME TO PRAY

Prayer of Salvation

If you have made it this far in reading this book and have not yet accepted Jesus Christ as your Lord and Savior, I want to extend this invitation to you. If you have already accepted Jesus Christ as your Lord and Savior, you may proceed to the next page.

You cannot experience a truly godly relationship without first having a relationship with your Heavenly Father. Love in Order begins with loving God first. When we surrender our lives to Him, He teaches us how to love ourselves, how to love others, and how to build relationships according to His design.

If you are ready to begin your relationship with the Lord today, I invite you to pray this prayer out loud:

Lord Jesus, I invite You into my life today.

Forgive me for my sins and cleanse my heart.
I believe that You died for me and rose again.

I accept You as my Lord and my Savior.

Write my name in the Book of Life

and lead me from this day forward,

Help me to walk in Your ways

and grow in my relationship with You.

In Jesus name, Amen.

If you prayed this prayer sincerely, welcome to the family of God. Your journey of healing, restoration, and walking in God's order has just begun. I encourage you to find a Bible-teaching, Holy Spirit–filled church where you can grow in your faith, learn God's Word, and be surrounded by a community that will support and strengthen your walk with the Lord.

Stay rooted in prayer, remain in the Word of God, and allow the Holy Spirit to guide you daily as you continue building your life and your relationships according to God's design.

Before You Pray

As I was preparing to send this book to print, the Holy Spirit woke me up at 2 a.m. and placed it strongly on my heart to add these prayers. I realized that these prayers are not only necessary for you, but also for the generations connected to you.

The Bible reminds us that our battles are not natural, but spiritual:

> "For we do not wrestle against flesh and blood, but against principalities, against powers, against the rulers of the darkness of this world, against spiritual wickedness in high places." Ephesians 6:12

Because of this, as you begin these spiritual warfare prayers, the Word of God instructs us to be prepared:

> "Put on the full armor of God, so that you can take your stand against the devil's schemes." Ephesians 6:11

As you put on the armor of God, remember that the Lord has already given you authority to stand against the enemy. We do not fight for victory; we fight from a place of victory, because Jesus Christ has already defeated the enemy through His death and resurrection.

So why do we still pray these prayers if Christ has already won the battle? Because at times generational patterns, unhealed wounds, and open doors can give the enemy access in areas where God has already given us authority. Prayer allows us to close those doors, renounce what does not belong in our lives, and stand fully in the power God has given us. Through Christ, we have been given the authority to overcome, the strength to stand, and the grace to walk in freedom.

Sometimes we carry burdens, wounds, and spiritual patterns from previous generations without even realizing it. The beginning of this book focused on healing and understanding the stages of love. This final section is dedicated to spiritual warfare prayers — prayers that help you reclaim what already belongs to you through Christ.

Allow the Holy Spirit to lead you as you pray. These written prayers are only a guide. As you pray them out loud, invite the Holy Spirit to reveal anything hidden, any area that needs healing, and any place where freedom is needed.

Stand in your God-given authority.
Pray with faith.
Pray with expectation.
And believe that God is restoring order in every area of your life.

Break The Spirit Of Fear

Fear is one of the enemy's most common tools. It can show up in many forms, fear of being alone, fear of failure, fear of rejection, fear that a spouse will leave or be unfaithful, or fear that the future will not work out. Whatever form fear takes, its goal is the same: to paralyze faith, distort love, and interfere with God's purpose.

Fear affects how we think, how we trust, and how we relate to others. When fear goes unaddressed, it can quietly influence decisions, create insecurity in relationships, and keep the heart guarded in unhealthy ways. Scripture makes it clear that fear does not come from God. Fear brings torment, but God brings peace, freedom, and security.

Through Jesus Christ, we are invited to walk in power, love, and a sound mind. These prayer points are meant to help identify fear honestly, release it fully, and invite God's perfect love to take its place.

> "For God has not given us a spirit of fear, but of power and of love and of a sound mind."
> 2 Timothy 1:7

> "For you did not receive the spirit of bondage again to fear, but you received the Spirit of adoption by whom we cry out, 'Abba, Father.'"
> Romans 8:15

1. Father God, I come before You as Your child, acknowledging that You are my protector and my source of peace.

2. I repent for allowing fear to influence my thoughts, emotions, and decisions.

3. I renounce and break every spirit of fear operating in my life.

4. I reject fear of being alone and declare that You will never leave me nor forsake me.

5. I break fear of failure and declare that my steps are ordered by the Lord.

6. I renounce fear of rejection and receive my identity and security in Christ.

7. I break fear that my spouse will leave me or be unfaithful.

8. I reject fear that my relationships will not last or will end in pain.

9. I break fear of abandonment rooted in past wounds or trauma.

10. I reject fear of the future and place my trust fully in You, Lord.

11. I renounce fear of people, opinions, and the need for approval.

12. I break fear that has caused me to guard my heart in unhealthy ways.

13. I declare that fear will no longer control how I love or trust.

14. I receive the Spirit of power, love, and a sound mind.

15. I choose faith over fear in every area of my life.

16. I ask You, Lord, to heal the root of fear operating in my heart.

17. I declare that anxiety, worry, and torment have no authority over me.

18. I place my life, my relationships, and my future into Your hands.

19. I thank You, Lord, that perfect love casts out all fear.

20. I walk forward in freedom, peace, and confidence in You.

In Jesus name, Amen.

Bloodlines and Generational Sexual Curses

Scripture teaches that patterns of sin, brokenness, and trauma can travel through family lines when they remain unaddressed. Sexual sin, abuse, exposure to pornography, and relationships outside of God's design often leave lasting effects, not only on individuals, but across generations.

When sexual boundaries are violated through abuse, molestation, or exploitation, the consequences can carry shame, confusion, and broken identity. Likewise, sexual activity outside of marriage, including pornography, creates unhealthy attachments that join the soul to what God never intended.

These patterns do not define a person, but they do require healing. God's heart is to redeem bloodlines, restore identity, and break cycles that were passed down through sin, trauma, or deception. Through repentance, forgiveness, and surrender to Jesus Christ, generational curses can be broken and replaced with blessing.

This section invites the reader to acknowledge family patterns honestly, without shame and to allow God to cleanse, heal, and realign their lineage according to His design.

1. Father God, I come before You as Your child, acknowledging that You are holy, righteous, and merciful.

2. I renounce and repent on behalf of my bloodline and myself for all who entered into sexual activity outside of marriage.

3. I repent for every generation that participated in sexual immorality, knowingly or unknowingly.

4. I ask You, Lord, to break the consequences of sexual abuse, molestation, and exploitation that entered my family line.

5. Heal every victim in my bloodline who suffered sexual trauma and restore what was stolen from them.

6. I repent for the use of pornography and any form of sexual satisfaction that replaced intimacy with You.

7. I acknowledge that ungodly sexual activity created unhealthy soul connections, and I ask You to sever them completely.

8. In the name of Jesus Christ, I renounce every generational curse tied to sexual sin, abuse, or perversion.

9. I declare that the power of the blood of Jesus speaks a better word over my family line.

10. Lord, remove me from every ungodly influence passed down through my family.

11. Establish me in a new, Godly covenant according to Your truth and Your Word.

12. I ask You to restore healthy identity, boundaries, and purpose in my life.

13. I renounce every mindset rooted in shame, secrecy, religion, legalism, or condemnation.

14. I reject every belief system that contradicts the truth of who I am in Christ.

15. I choose freedom over bondage and truth over deception.

16. I declare that my household belongs to the Lord.

17. I call my family line into alignment with Your kingdom purposes.

18. I place my trust fully in Jesus Christ, the victorious Son of God.

19. I receive healing, cleansing, and restoration through the blood of Jesus.
20. Thank You, Lord, for breaking cycles and establishing generational blessing.

In Jesus name, Amen.

Understanding Soul Ties

A *soul tie* is a deep emotional, spiritual, or relational bond formed between two people. Soul ties are not always negative, God designed healthy soul ties to exist in relationships such as marriage, family, and godly friendships. Scripture describes this kind of connection as unity of heart and purpose.

However, soul ties can become ungodly when they are formed outside of God's design, especially through:

- Sexual relationships outside of covenant

- Emotional dependency

- Trauma bonds

- Manipulation or control

- Relationships rooted in lust, fear, or insecurity

Ungodly soul ties can keep a person emotionally connected to someone God has already removed, making it difficult to move forward in healing, purity, and healthy relationships. These ties often affect thoughts, emotions, desires, and decision-making long after the relationship has ended.

God's desire is not to leave us fragmented, but whole. Through repentance, forgiveness, and surrender, the Lord is able to break unhealthy soul ties and restore the heart into proper order.

Prayer Points to Break Ungodly Soul Ties

1. Father God, I come before You as Your child, acknowledging that You are my Father, my Healer, and the God who restores my soul.

2. I repent for forming emotional or sexual connections outside of Your will for my life.

3. Forgive me, Lord, for every ungodly soul tie formed through relationships that did not honor You.

4. Wash me with the blood of Jesus and cleanse my heart from every unhealthy attachment.

5. In the name of Jesus, I renounce and break every ungodly soul tie connected to my past.

6. I release every person I have been emotionally, sexually, or spiritually tied to outside of covenant.

7. I forgive those who have wounded me, used me, or formed unhealthy bonds with me.

8. I receive Your healing in every place where my heart was fragmented or wounded.

9. Restore my emotions, my desires, and my affections back to wholeness.

10. I break every tie rooted in lust, manipulation, control, fear, or insecurity.

11. I declare that my soul belongs fully to You, Lord.

12. Heal every trauma bond and emotional dependency formed through past relationships.

13. I ask You, Holy Spirit, to fill every space that was once occupied by unhealthy connections.

14. I choose freedom over familiarity and healing over attachment.

15. Restore my heart so that I can love again in a healthy, God-honoring way.

16. I declare that my love will be formed in wisdom, purity, and order.

17. I receive Your peace, clarity, and restoration.

18. Thank You, Lord, for making me whole again.

19. I ask You, Lord, to restore every part of my heart that was weakened through unhealthy attachment.

20. I declare that my soul is healed, my emotions are stable, and my future relationships will be formed in wisdom, freedom, and God's order.

In Jesus name, Amen.

Incubus and Succubus

These spirits are unwanted sexual dreams, intrusive nighttime experiences, or recurring patterns of sexual temptation that occur while a person is asleep. Such experiences are sometimes referred to as spirit husbands or spirit wives, describing counterfeit forms of intimacy that operate outside of God's design for covenant and purity.

- Incubus meaning *"to lie upon."* It is a male spirit that shows up in female dreams to target women through sexual dreams or nighttime encounters.

- Succubus meaning *"to lie under."* It is a female spirit that shows up in male dreams to target men through sexual dreams or nighttime encounters.

While these specific descriptions are not named directly in Scripture, they are commonly discussed in the context of spiritual warfare, temptation of the flesh, and the vulnerability of the mind during sleep. This understanding brings awareness to the importance of inviting God's protection into every area of our lives, including our dreams.

If you have experienced sexual encounters in your dreams with someone, this is often described in spiritual warfare language as an incubus or succubus attack. These attacks are spiritual encounters associated with sexual activity occurring during sleep, where the presence appears in dreams with the intent of engaging a person in sexual activity. This awareness is shared so that you remain alert, prayerful, and grounded in the authority given through Jesus Christ.

Prayer Points to Break Incubus and Succubus Spirits

1. Lord, I come before You as Your child, acknowledging that You are my Father, my Healer, and the God who restores all things.

2. I repent for any open doors I have given to incubus, succubus, or any ungodly sexual spirit.

3. Forgive me, Lord, for any past ungodly sexual relationships that were outside of Your will.

4. Wash me with Your blood and make me clean and pure again, not only in my body, but also in my mind.

5. In the name of Jesus, I renounce and break every agreement with incubus, succubus, and every ungodly sexual spirit.

6. I declare that my body is the temple of the Holy Spirit and belongs fully to You.

7. Lord, cleanse my dreams and remove anything that is not from You.

8. I come against every recurring or intrusive sexual dream that brings confusion, shame, or bondage.

9. I declare that my dreams will align with Your truth, Your peace, and Your purpose.

10. I break every counterfeit form of intimacy operating in my life that is outside of Your design.

11. Heal every wound in my heart that has contributed to unhealthy desire.

12. I reject every sexual spirit that attempts to operate through my dreams.

13. Holy Spirit, cover my mind and heart with Your protection.

14. I declare that no ungodly spirit has permission to access my life, my thoughts, or my dreams.

15. I receive Your healing, freedom, and restoration.

16. Thank You, Lord, for restoring order to my life and my relationships.

17. I declare that my love is healed, my heart is guarded, and my life belongs fully to You.

18. I stand in the authority given to me through Jesus Christ and walk forward in freedom.

19. I declare that every door opened through fear, curiosity, or lack of knowledge is now closed by the authority of Jesus Christ.

20. I thank You, Lord, that my life is sealed, covered, and governed by the Holy Spirit, and that I walk forward in purity, peace, and freedom.

In Jesus name, Amen.

Prayer Of Covering

As we close these prayer points, I am reminded to guard my heart, walk in alignment with the Holy Spirit, and remain obedient to what the Lord instructs. Your Word reminds us that the enemy comes to steal, kill, and destroy, but You, Lord, have come to give life, and life more abundantly.

Father, thank You for Your protection, Your mercy, and Your faithfulness over my life. Thank You for every door You have closed that was not meant for me, and for every path You have opened according to Your will. I thank You that I am washed and made clean by the blood of Jesus.

Lord, guard my heart, guard my relationships, and keep me aligned with Your will. Help me to walk daily in wisdom, obedience, and spiritual awareness. Guide my steps and keep me grounded in Your truth. I declare that I will see the goodness of the Lord in the land of the living, and I will walk forward in faith, peace, and confidence in Your promises.

Thank You, Lord, for covering my life, my family, and my future.
In Jesus' name, Amen.

TESTIMONIES: STORIES THROUGH THE STAGES

HOW COUPLES WALKED FROM FRIENDSHIP TO COVENANT

Testimony 1 — Sammy & Jasline
"How the 5 Stages Helped Us Build a Strong Marriage"

Our story didn't begin with romance, it began with friendship.
More than twenty years ago, Benny and Thalia were our youth
leaders. We were all part of small groups: the men gathered with
Benny, and the women gathered with Thalia. That's how our
friendship started, not just with them, but with each other.
For four years, we were simply friends. And honestly, we are
grateful we didn't rush past that stage.

During those years, we learned each other's character. We served in
church together. We saw how each of us handled pressure,
responsibility, and life. There was no pretending, no performing ,
just genuine connection. Looking back, we now realize that God
used those four years to protect our hearts and prepare a strong
foundation.

When Feelings Began to Grow

Somewhere along the journey, something shifted , especially for
Sammy. But Jasline wasn't ready to move out of the friendship
stage yet. She valued what we had, and she wanted to be certain
that if we stepped into something deeper, it would be God-led, not
emotion-led. So instead of rushing, we prayed. We sought wise
counsel. We waited.

That's when the stages began to make sense for us, even before
they had names.

Transitioning Into "Friends in Love"

We stepped into this stage slowly, carefully, and prayerfully. Our feelings were growing, but we didn't want to confuse emotion with confirmation. We protected the friendship while exploring whether God was opening the door to something deeper.

As this stage developed, Sammy was ready to move into courtship, but Jasline wasn't there yet. Outside voices were bringing confusion, making it difficult to discern clearly.

One day, during a car ride conversation with Thalia, Jasline shared everything, the feelings, the confusion, and the fear of making the wrong decision. Thalia lovingly told her:"You need to listen to God, not people." That moment brought clarity.

Stage 3: Courtship

Once we both felt peace, we entered courtship. This stage required intentionality, boundaries, prayer, honest conversations, and accountability. Benny and Thalia walked beside us with wisdom and care. They didn't control our relationship; they guided us.

Courtship helped us:
- communicate honestly
- set healthy expectations
- identify our emotional triggers
- strengthen our faith
- and move forward with clarity instead of confusion

Stage 4: Engagement

Our engagement was beautiful. It happened upstate New York during a youth retreat, and Thalia and Benny were there to witness it. By the time we got engaged, our foundation was strong. We weren't guessing, hoping, or forcing anything, we knew what God had spoken. Engagement brought its own challenges: stress, planning, disagreements, and learning how to blend our ideas. But the earlier stages kept us united. Even in moments of conflict, we knew God was with us.

Stage 5: Marriage

At the time of this writing, we have been married 13 years.
God has blessed us with three beautiful children and two successful businesses. If God did it for us, He can do it for you.
Our marriage hasn't been perfect, but it has been purposeful.
Years of growth.
Years of forgiveness.
Years of unity and joy.

These stages helped us:
- build slowly
- build wisely
- and build on God's timing, not our emotions

We are living proof that when you follow God's order, He blesses the outcome. If you take anything from our story, let it be this:
Do not rush. Do not skip stages.
Let God write the story.
His timing is worth the wait.

With love,
Sammy & Jasline

Testimony 2 — Eddy & Inez
"Obedience Opened the Door to God's Best for Us"

When I (Eddy) first came to church, I was already in a relationship. At that time, I came under the leadership of Benny and Thalia, we called them *Pop* and *Mom* because they shepherded us like spiritual parents. We were part of the same small group, and that's how our journey with them began.

As I grew spiritually, I knew I needed guidance about the relationship I was in. I went to Pop (Benny) for counsel many times because the relationship was unstable. We had already crossed boundaries, we kept breaking up and getting back together, and deep down, I knew it was not God's will, but the emotional soul tie made it extremely hard to let go. Pop told me, in love and truth: "Son, you need to let this go so you can focus on God."

It wasn't easy to hear.
It wasn't easy to obey.
But it was necessary.

That relationship was built on lust, not purpose. At the time, I honestly believed I wouldn't be able to survive without that person, that's how strong the soul tie was. But once I surrendered, God began to heal my heart, renew my mind, and break the things that were never from Him. During this time, Inez and I were simply friends.
We were around each other because we were in the same ministry,

the same small group, and the same community. There was no pressure, no forcing, no rushing, just genuine friendship.

As I focused on God and allowed Him to reorder my life, something began to shift quietly and naturally. God began working in our hearts. Feelings awakened slowly, safely, and with peace. We started walking through the stages Benny and Thalia had taught us, friendship, friends in love, courtship, and eventually engagement.

Those stages protected us. They healed us. They aligned us.
Today, we can say with confidence: Obedience opened the door to God's best.

At the time of this writing, we have been married 12 years and God has blessed us with two beautiful children. Looking back, we thank God we did things His way. Letting go felt impossible at the time, but it was the best decision we ever made. What I thought I couldn't live without was actually the very thing blocking the blessing God had for me.

If you take anything from our story, let it be this:
Before the blessing, the enemy will always send a distraction, even a counterfeit.

Choose obedience. Choose God's voice.
What God has for you is worth every step of surrender.

With love,
Eddie & Inez

Testimony 3 — Angel & Maria
"A Marriage That Made Every Season Worth It"

I didn't grow up with the perfect background.
I was a guy from the streets, rough, broken, and far from God.
But when the Lord redirected my life, everything changed.

When Maria and I met, we chose to hoIf you take anything with
you from these pages, let it be this: God cares deeply about how
you love, who you love, and the order in which you love. When
you choose His way, even when it feels slow, uncomfortable, or
countercultural, you position yourself for a love story that is not
only beautiful, but enduring. nor God from the beginning.

We followed the stages, friendship, friends in love, courtship,
engagement, and marriage. We faced challenges like any other
couple, but we walked through each stage with prayer, faith, and
the wisdom Benny and Thalia poured into us.

God blessed our marriage. But after 13 years together, my wife
Maria passed away from cancer.

Losing her was the hardest thing I have ever faced. Even now, it
hurts. She was my partner, my answered prayer, my blessing from
God. But even in the middle of grief, I can say this with confidence:
God is still good. Following the stages doesn't mean life will be
perfect.

It doesn't mean storms won't come. It doesn't mean you won't experience pain.
But it *does* mean you will build something real.
Something strong. Something worth fighting for.

I thank God for the years He gave me with Maria
For the love we shared.
For the growth we experienced.
For the covenant we made.
For the home we built together.

Our story is proof that even when life brings heartbreak, God's faithfulness remains. What I want every couple to know is that they should do everything God's way because it's worth it. Even when life takes a turn you never expected, His grace will carry you.

With gratitude,
Angel

CLOSING REFLECTIONS

YOUR LOVE STORY HAS A DESIGNER
This journey is not just about romance, it is about purpose.

Whether you are single, dating, engaged, newly married, or decades into covenant, God is still writing your story. He is not finished with you yet.

God is the author of your story. He is the one who writes every season, aligns every connection, softens every heart, and orders every step. Nothing in your journey is random. Nothing is wasted. Every moment, every delay, every lesson is held in His hands.

He is the one who teaches patience in friendship, purity as emotions awaken, intentionality in courtship, wisdom in engagement, and unity in marriage. Each stage is carefully designed to prepare your heart for the next, shaping you into someone who can love well and love wisely.

God strengthens you through spiritual warfare, refines you through covenant, and empowers you to love; not with your own strength, but with His heart. When you feel stretched, challenged, or unsure, remember that He is forming something deeper within you. And because He is the Designer, you can trust His timing. You can trust His process. You can trust His voice above every other voice. Your love story is not being rushed. It is being written by God Himself.

One of the most important truths I want you to remember is this: no relationship is perfect, at any stage. Don't strive for perfection.

Pursue a healthy relationship, one rooted in growth, mature and one that evolves over time.

THE TRUTH I PRAY YOU REMEMBER

If you remember nothing else from this book, remember this:

- God is faithful in every stage

- He is present in friendship, guarding your heart and shaping your foundation.

- He is gentle in the *friends in love stage.* He'll teach you how to steward emotions with wisdom and purity.

- He is guiding you in courtship, bringing clarity where feelings deepen.

- He is confirming His will in engagement, aligning purpose and direction.

- He is uniting hearts in marriage, forming a covenant under His hand.

- He is strengthening you in conflict, teaching you how to love with grace.

- He is refining you through covenant, shaping you into His image.

- And He is blessing every step of obedience.

What God begins, He completes. What He ordains, He protects. What He joins together, no one can separate.

Your role is not to strive, but to remain faithful.
Stay surrendered.
Stay prayerful.
Stay united.
Stay anchored in God's will.
When you do, you will never walk alone. The author of your love story is walking with you, every step of the way.

God is not just preparing you for a relationship. He is preparing *you*. He is shaping your character, refining your heart, and teaching you how to love with wisdom, purity, patience, and spiritual maturity. He is teaching you how to hear His voice, honor His order, and trust His timing.

Because love is not built in a moment. It is built in stages.
It is strengthened through obedience. And it is sustained by God.

Trusting God With Your Love Story

As you come to the end of this book, pause for a moment and take a deep breath. Look back at what you have walked through. Look at what God has revealed to you along the way. Look at the strength He has been building in you, quietly, intentionally, faithfully, through every stage.

On this journey, you should move from friendship, to friends in love, to courtship, to engagement, and finally into the sacred covenant of marriage. Each stage carries its own beauty. Each stage brings its own challenges. Each stage requires growth, obedience, and trust. And in every one of them, God is present.

None of these stages are accidental.
None of them are wasted.
Every season matters.
Every step has a purpose.

Your journey does not end here.
It continues, one prayer, one conversation, one choice at a time.
And as long as you keep God at the center, you will never walk alone.

If you take anything with you from these pages, let it be this: God cares deeply about how you love, who you love, and the order in which you love. When you choose His way—even when it feels slow, uncomfortable, or countercultural—you position yourself for a love story that is not only beautiful, but healthy, resilient, and enduring.

God Redeems What Was Skipped

Before you close this book, I want you to hear this clearly and without shame, it does not matter if your journey did not follow the stages in order.

Maybe you skipped stages.
Maybe things moved faster than they should have.
Maybe life happened before clarity came.
Perhaps you skipped engagement and moved in together.
Perhaps marriage was delayed and children came before covenant.
Perhaps you are already deep into a relationship that didn't begin the way you hoped.

Hear this truth with grace: *God is not limited by timeline.*

We serve a God who redeems time, He lives outside of time. He restores what was rushed, heals what was broken, cleanses what was misaligned, and makes all things new. If something was skipped, the Lord is not saying, *"It's too late.* He is telling you, **"Go Back And Do It AGAIN "**

God is a God of order, and He is always willing to step into chaos to bring alignment. Throughout Scripture, we see this again and again. Our Heavenly Father calms storms, restores what is broken, and brings dead things back to life. He specializes in redemption. He is not intimidated by disorder, delay, or mistakes.

God does not only calm storms—He gives instructions in the middle of them. When we obey, He brings things back into divine order.

What feels chaotic can become aligned.
What feels delayed can be redeemed.
What feels broken can be made new.

He is a God who restores, reorders, and realigns hearts that are surrendered to Him.

To The Man Reading This....
I want to speak to you clearly, and with honor.

You are called to lead, not just with words, but with obedience. God has entrusted you with responsibility, covering, and courage. Leadership in God's Kingdom is not about control, it is about sacrifice, accountability, and covenant. If God has joined your hearts, do not delay obedience. If you have not honored the stage of engagement, this is your moment. Get on one knee. Ask her to be your wife. Cover her with covenant. Not because culture demands it, but because God does. If you are living together without marriage, even if you are engaged, even if you share children, do not ignore God's order. Love without covenant leaves a woman uncovered and a man unaligned. God's design is not restrictive; it is protective.

A man of God does not consume what he refuses to commit to.
A man of God does not delay obedience. When clarity has already been given
A man of God does not lead a woman into compromise, he leads her into covering.

This is not about pressure.
This is about alignment.
When you choose obedience, God honors it.
When you step into covenant, God supplies grace.
When you lead with integrity, God strengthens your hands.

Do not fear doing God's way.
Do not wait for the "perfect time."
And don't allow comfort to replace obedience.If you love her,
honor her. If you see a future with her, cover her.

The enemy does not play fair. He looks for open doors, small
compromises, delayed obedience, unfinished stages, and
half-commitments, to disrupt what God is building. The devil
does not need permission; he looks for access. And access is often
created when obedience is postponed.

But when you choose to obey, those doors close.
When you walk in alignment, confusion loses its power.
When you honor God's design, His protection surrounds what
you build.

Leadership begins with obedience.
Covering begins with covenant.
And when a man chooses to do it God's way, God responds with
grace, strength, and favor to sustain what He has entrusted to you.
This is not about pressure. This is about responsibility, honor, and
legacy. And God will honor the man who honors His order.

To The Woman Reading This....
I want to speak to you with truth and love.

You are the daughter of the Most High God.
His masterpiece, created with intention, dignity, and purpose. Your value does not come from a relationship, a title, or a season of life, it comes from The God who created you.

If you find yourself in a relationship that displeases God's order, silences the Holy Spirit, or asks you to compromise what you know is right, this is your invitation to pause and listen. This is not about shame. This is not about condemnation. This is about alignment.

Honoring God with your body, soul, and mind matters. Obedience is not punishment, it is protection. When you choose to honor the Holy Spirit, even when it feels uncomfortable or costly, God honors your obedience. He sees your heart. He responds to surrender.

I am not telling you to walk away in fear.
I am telling you to walk forward in obedience.

God is faithful to redeem, restore, and reorder what has been out of alignment. When you choose His way, He steps in with grace, and clarity. You do not lose by obeying God, you gain direction, and favor.

Read this aloud:
I am not behind.
I am not disqualified.
I am not forgotten.
I am loved.
I am chosen.
I am worth to be honored

I often tell my spiritual and natural daughters; "**Hide** yourself in the presence of God, so that in order for a man to find you, he must first find the Lord."

The word hide means to conceal To hide yourself in the presence of God means no one has easy access to you. No one gets your heart without seeking God first. They must come through God's presence to find you.

When a woman hides herself in God, she is not hidden from Purpose—she is **covered**.
She is not overlooked—she is **protected**.
She is not delayed—she is being **prepared**.

A man of God will not try to bypass God to reach you.
He will seek God's heart first, and in doing so, he will be led to your heart. This is God's protection over His daughters.
It is how He preserves purity, guards the heart, and ensures that love is found in order, not confusion. Hide yourself in Him and trust God to decide who is worthy of finding you.

BONUS CONTENT:

I. **RELATIONSHIP READINESS SELF-ASSESSMENT**

II. **SETTING GODLY BOUNDARIES**

III. **DISCUSSION QUESTIONS FOR INDIVIDUALS, COUPLES, AND GROUPS**

IV. **WEDDING HOME PREPARATION CHECKLIST**

I. Relationship Readiness Self-Assessment
A personal reflection tool, not a test

Just in case you are in a season of waiting, discerning, or preparing for what God may be building in your life, I wanted to leave you with this bonus, a Relationship Readiness Self-Assessment.

Before God brings two people together, He often does a deep work within each individual. When I was learning about relationships and God's design for love, I realized how important it was to pause and honestly assess my heart, my healing, and my readiness for covenant. This self-assessment is not meant to judge you or rush you. It is meant to help you see clearly where you are and invite God into the places that still need growth.

This is not a test you pass or fail. It is a reflection tool. Some questions may affirm how far you've come. Others may gently reveal areas where God wants to heal, mature, or prepare you more deeply.

If you are not pursuing a relationship right now, that's okay. This is still valuable. You can use it to better understand yourself, to grow emotionally and spiritually, or to prepare for a future season God has not yet revealed. Wisdom gained early often protects us later.

My prayer is that this self-assessment helps you walk forward with honesty, peace, and confidence, trusting that God is faithful to prepare you for the love He desires for you.

This self-assessment is designed to help you pause, pray, and honestly evaluate where you are before God in your relationship journey. There are no right or wrong answers. The goal is awareness, alignment, and growth.

Answer each question honestly. If something feels uncomfortable, that may be an area God wants to heal or strengthen.

Spiritual Readiness
- I regularly seek God through prayer and Scripture.

- I desire a relationship that honors God more than my own comfort.

- I am willing to wait on God's timing rather than rush ahead.

- My faith does not depend on a relationship to feel complete.

Emotional Readiness
- I have processed past heartbreak, trauma, or loss.
- I do not look to another person to fix my pain.
- I can communicate my feelings in a healthy way.
- I take responsibility for my emotional reactions.

Identity and Wholeness
- I know who I am apart from being in a relationship.
- I do not compromise my values to be chosen.
- I feel secure being single if God asks me to wait.
- My worth is rooted in Christ, not in validation from others.

Relationship Patterns

- I recognize unhealthy patterns from my past.
- I am willing to do relationships differently if God leads me to.
- I respond to conflict with maturity rather than avoidance or anger.
- I can receive correction without becoming defensive.

Readiness for Covenant

- I understand marriage as a covenant, not just a feeling.
- I am willing to sacrifice for the good of another.
- I am open to accountability and spiritual leadership.
- I am committed to building something lasting, not temporary.

II. Setting Godly Boundaries
Protection, not punishment

Just in case you are navigating attraction, emotional connection, or the desire for love, I wanted to leave you with this bonus: a guide to setting God-honoring boundaries.

Boundaries are often misunderstood. They are not walls meant to keep people out, and they are not rules meant to restrict joy. Boundaries are gifts from God that protect your heart, your peace, and your future. They create space for trust to grow, for love to mature, and for obedience to remain intact.

I know from experience how easy it is to let emotions lead before wisdom catches up. This guide is here to help you slow down, reflect, and choose boundaries that align with God's design rather than cultural pressure or fear of losing someone.

Whether you are single, dating, courting, engaged, or even married, boundaries matter in every stage. They help keep relationships healthy, respectful, and rooted in God's order.

If you are unsure where to start, begin with prayer. Ask God to show you where boundaries are needed, not to take something away from you, but to protect something sacred.

My prayer is that this guide helps you choose obedience with confidence and love with clarity.

Boundaries are not about control. They are about clarity, safety, and obedience. Godly boundaries protect your heart, your faith, and your future.

1. **Emotional Boundaries**
   Healthy emotional boundaries mean:

   - Not oversharing too quickly.
   - Not using someone to fill loneliness.
     Not placing emotional dependence on a person instead of God.
   - Allowing trust to grow with time and consistency.

   Ask yourself:
   Am I sharing my heart wisely, or prematurely?

2. **Physical Boundaries**
   Physical boundaries should reflect your desire to honor God. This includes:
   - Agreeing in advance on limits.
   - Avoiding situations that create unnecessary temptation.
   - Respecting your body and the other person's body as sacred.

   Ask yourself:
   Do my actions align with my faith, or just my feelings?

3. **Spiritual Boundaries**
   Spiritual intimacy is powerful and should not be rushed. Healthy practices include:

- Praying together with reverence, not manipulation.
- Not using Scripture to pressure or control.
- Making sure faith is shared, not just spoken.

Ask yourself:
Is God truly at the center of this relationship?

4. **Digital and Social Boundaries**
In today's world, boundaries also apply online. Consider:
- How often you communicate.
- What you post or share publicly.
- Whether social media creates comparison, jealousy, or insecurity.

Ask yourself:
Does this strengthen peace or create confusion?

III.   Discussion Questions for Individuals, Couples, and Groups

Just in case you want to go deeper, I wanted to leave you with this bonus,

a set of discussion questions to help you reflect, process, and grow beyond the pages of this book.

Sometimes the greatest transformation happens when we slow down and ask intentional questions. These discussion prompts are designed to help you examine your own heart, have meaningful conversations with a partner, or engage in thoughtful dialogue within a group setting.

You can use these questions on your own during journaling or prayer time. Couples can use them to strengthen communication and alignment. Small groups, book clubs, or premarital classes can use them to foster honest and encouraging conversations.

There is no pressure to answer every question. Let the Holy Spirit guide which ones you sit with longer. Growth is not rushed, and clarity often comes through reflection.

My prayer is that these questions help you gain wisdom, deepen understanding, and walk forward with greater intentionality in how you love. These questions can be used for personal reflection, couple conversations, book clubs, or small groups.

Personal Reflection

1. Which relationship stage challenged me the most and why?

2. Where do I see growth in how I love compared to my past?

3. What fears do I need to surrender to God?

4. Am I waiting well, or rushing out of fear?

5. What does God's design for love look like in my life right now?

For Couples

1. Which stage are we currently in and how are we honoring it?

2. How do we handle conflict and disagreement?

3. Where can we grow spiritually together?

4. Are our boundaries clear and respected?

5. What does covenant mean to us, not just marriage?

For Groups or Book Studies

1. How does culture differ from God's design for relationships?

2. Why is healing important before pursuing love?

3. What role does patience play in godly relationships?

4. How can we support one another in waiting or preparation?

5. What stood out most from the testimonies shared in this book?

IV.   Wedding & Home Preparation Checklist
Bonus Resource for Stage 4: Engagement

Just in case you are in this stage, I wanted to leave you with a special bonus: a Wedding and Home Preparation Checklist.

When I was preparing for marriage, I didn't have anything like this. I was learning as I went, figuring things out in real time, and wishing someone had handed me something practical to guide me. So I wanted to leave this here for you, to serve you, support you, and help you prepare with intention and peace.

This checklist is designed to help you think through both the wedding and the home you are building together, not just practically, but prayerfully. Marriage is more than a ceremony; it is the beginning of a shared life, a shared space, and a shared responsibility before God.

If you are not in this stage yet, that's okay. You can save this for the future, revisit it when the time comes, or even share it with someone else who is preparing for marriage. God often allows us to carry wisdom not only for ourselves, but for others as well.

My prayer is that this checklist helps you prepare with clarity, unity, and joy as you step into the covenant God is calling you into.

As you prepare for covenant, here is a practical guide to help you stay organized, peaceful, and intentional. Use this checklist as a tool, not a burden, as you steward the beautiful season God has entrusted to you.

Let this checklist remove stress, not create it. Let it serve you, not overwhelm you. And remember: the goal is not the wedding day... The goal is marriage.

Wedding Planning Essentials

Attire & Accessories

- Wedding dress
- Veil / hair accessories
- Jewelry
- Shoes
- Undergarments (shapewear, slip, etc.)
- Groom's suit or tuxedo
- Bridesmaids' dresses
- Groomsmen's suits
- Accessories for the bridal party

Photography & Media
- Photographer
- Videographer (optional but highly recommended)
- Engagement photoshoot (if desired)

Venue & Décor

- Ceremony venue
- Reception venue
- Decorations (table settings, centerpieces, drapery, etc.)
- Flowers: bouquets, boutonnieres, centerpieces
- Lighting, candles, aisle décor

Invitations & Stationery

- Save-the-date cards
- Wedding invitations
- RSVP cards
- Ceremony programs
- Menu cards (optional)
- Place cards
- Thank-you notes

Catering & Cake

- Catering service (food + beverages)
- Wedding cake or dessert table
- Cake topper (optional)
- Cutting set / plates & utensils

Entertainment

- DJ or live band
- Ceremony music playlist
- Reception playlist (first dance, parent dances, etc.)

Ceremony & Legal Requirements

- Officiant
- Marriage license

- Vows (if writing personal ones)
- Ring bearer pillow / flower girl basket
- Wedding rings

Logistics & Extras
- Wedding planner / coordinator (optional)
- Day-of timeline
- Transportation (limo, classic car, etc.)
- Guest favors
- Welcome table / guestbook
- Seating chart
- Emergency bridal kit (pins, makeup, band-aids, etc.)

Honeymoon Preparation
- Flight tickets
- Hotel reservations
- Car rental (if needed)
- Itinerary
- Passports / IDs
- Luggage essentials

HOME ESSENTIALS FOR NEWLYWEDS
Marriage begins with building a home—whether big or small, simple or detailed. Here are foundational essentials to help you start with order and peace.

Bedroom Essentials
- Bed frame & mattress
- Pillows (2–4) & Sheet set
- Comforter or duvet

- Nightstands
- Dresser or closet organizers
- Lamps or bedside lighting
- Curtains or blinds

Bathroom Essentials
- Towels (hand, bath, face)
- Bath mat
- Shower curtain & hooks
- Toilet paper & holders
- Cleaning supplies (brush, disinfectant, wipes)
- Toiletry storage
- Trash can

Laundry Essentials
- Washer & dryer (if not provided)
- Laundry detergent
- Fabric softener (optional)
- Iron & ironing board
- Laundry basket or hampers

Living Room & Dining Area
- Sofa / couch
- Coffee table
- TV & TV stand
- Additional seating
- Dining table & chairs
- Throw pillows / blankets

Kitchen Essentials

- Refrigerator, stove, microwave (if not included)
- Pots & pans
- Cooking utensils
- Dishes & silverware
- Cups, mugs, glasses
- Cutting boards & knives
- Food storage containers
- Trash can & bags
- Basic spices & pantry items

Cleaning & Organization

- Mop, broom, vacuum
- All-purpose cleaner
- Dish soap & sponges
- Shelving or storage bins
- Tool kit (hammer, screwdriver, etc.)
- Light bulbs

How to Use This Checklist

- Pray first. Let God guide what matters for your wedding and home.
- Don't rush. You do not need everything all at once.
- Stay unified. Make decisions together as a team.
- Stay peaceful. This is not about perfection, it's about preparation.
- Stay grateful. You are building a life that God has blessed.

SPECIAL ACKNOWLEDGMENT

Acknowledgments

I want to take a moment to honor two very special people who unknowingly sparked the revival of these principles in my heart, my beautiful daughter, Gaby, and my future son-in-love, Joshua.

At the time of writing this book, the two of you are in Stage Three: Courtship, walking with intention, humility, and a deep desire to honor God. When you came to us to share your hearts, to seek guidance, on how to navigate your relationship God's way, it brought back so many memories of the stages your father and I once walked through.

Those conversations reminded me of God's faithfulness, how He guided, protected and corrected us along the way. As we shared wisdom with you both, the Holy Spirit stirred those same truths within me again and made me realize something powerful: The next generation needs this.

To Our Beautiful Daughter, Gaby:

Thank you for your openness, your maturity, and the honor you show us. Watching you grow into a woman of strength, compassion, and faith has been one of my greatest joys. Thank you for asking me almost every day, *"Mom, when are you going to finish this book?"* Every time you asked, it carried me through moments when I wanted to quit. God used you to confirm that this book needed to be born.

To Our Future Son-In-Love, Josh (AkA fafa)

Thank you for your respect, sincerity, and your desire to seek God first. Your humility and your commitment to honoring our daughter reflect true godly character, and we are deeply grateful for you. You are truly an answered prayer. From watching you grow up during family visits, to becoming my husband's barber, and now stepping into the role of our future son-in-love, only the Lord could have written this story. God certainly has a sense of humor! None of us saw this coming, but He did. We are honored to call you our son and wouldn't have it any other way.

You both reminded me that the lessons God taught us were never meant to stay with just one generation, they were meant to be passed down, shared, and lived out. I know the Lord will walk with you through every stage. Keep Him first, listen to His voice, and protect the beautiful covenant He is preparing.

I love you both dearly.
Mom

About the Author

About the Author

Thalia N. Alvarez is a wife, mother, mentor, and faith leader with a deep passion for helping individuals and couples build healthy, God-centered relationships. Alongside her husband of over two decades, she has walked through every stage of relationship, friendship, friends in love, courtship, engagement, and marriage,learning firsthand the beauty, challenges, and refining power of God's design for love.

With years of experience counseling couples, mentoring young adults, and serving in ministry, Thalia has seen how many relationships struggle not because of a lack of love, but because of a lack of understanding, order, and spiritual foundation. Her heart is to bring clarity, healing, and biblical wisdom to relationships, helping people avoid unnecessary heartbreak and walk in God's timing with confidence and peace. Thalia writes from a place of lived experience, spiritual discernment, and deep compassion. She believes that love is not meant to be rushed, confused, or built on emotion alone, but guided by God, grounded in wisdom, and strengthened through obedience. Her teaching style blends truth with grace, pastoral insight with practical guidance, and faith with real-life application.

Above all, Thalia's desire is that every reader would come to know God as the true Author of their love story, and trust Him to write it beautifully, one stage at a time.

9 798994 237526